122 Conversations:

Person to Person, Art Beyond Borders

Anne Labovitz

Black suitcase with white Tyvek® bag, 2017, 26" by 18" by 10". Suitcase was photographed before transportation and contains the entire exhibition for Rania, Iraqi Kurdistan, weighing no more than 45 pounds.

Table of Contents

Inspired by Växjö for Duluth, 2018
Acrylic on Tyvek®
Diptych 501.5" by 30" (left), 596.5" by 30" (right)
Anne Labovitz

Ken Bloom

The Tweed Museum mission is to bring art and people of our communities together for delight, for discovery, and for learning. Along with maintaining and enhancing the Museum's art collection and promoting visual art as a vital form of communication, the Tweed is an active participant in a vibrant cultural community where collective programming can provide unparalleled experiences for audiences. Art can bridge social divides by stirring the mind to understanding in ways that words may not. The work of humanistically oriented artists in dialogue with their audiences offer pathways to mutual understanding and especially, compassion. This collaborative program, led by the artist Anne Labovitz, seeks to accomplish that goal.

In an essay on what it means to be human, Chinese dissident artist Ai Weiwei writes, "Everything hangs on how we define ourselves and how we treat those with whom we share our surroundings, which are teeming with different ethnicities, religions and cultures."

May I introduce you to a project very close to my heart as well as to the mission of the Tweed?

The six-year project, *122 Conversations: Person to Person, Art Beyond Borders* was inspired by Labovitz's impulse to work in a social sphere engaging with a participating audience in a cross-cultural dialogue, which would result in a form blurred in its distinctions between author and audience. Labovitz's vision was to establish connections with the participants and then to render the dialogue by artistic means. Representing numerous conversations in the form of encrypted scripts, embedded within polychromatic layers of paint and resin, Labovitz transformed the experiences of cross-cultural dialogue into visual forms and then invited the many participants to share their own pictorial responses.

According to Darsie Alexander, an essayist in this catalog, "giving material form to a psychological state or emotion is a daunting challenge for any artist." Yet, this is precisely what was required of Labovitz to accomplish the goals of the project.

By conducting and recording the person-to-person interviews and engaging with participants on a personal level, Labovitz initiated trusting relationships. These conversations became root sources of inspiration for the artworks of the project, which were at first formal paintings. As the project progressed, the form of the paintings changed into long scrolls (which elicit a sculptural bearing in the gallery).

Each Labovitz artwork depicts an interpretative vision of the collective interactions from each city. And the people drew archetypal figures, wrote poetic phrases, and offered affirmations of the program themes, from the perspective of their city. These were elements brought to mind through cross-cultural conversation, then inscribed within artwork, and embedded, layer under layer.

From 2015 to 2018, each Sister City hosted an exhibition of the Labovitz artworks. To extend the participatory nature of the project, multiple elements of the exhibition encouraged creative engagement with guests according to participatory opportunities organized by the artist. More than 3,000 people added to the project by creating works by writing, mark-making, and drawing on paper sheets prepared for each venue by Labovitz. The imagery of these intimate artworks, ranging from the vernacular to the abstract, all embody the humanist message. The culminating exhibition at the Tweed presents representative elements of the entire project, including Labovitz's paintings, participatory artworks from each venue, photographs, video, and documentation.

122 Conversations was founded upon acknowledging and demonstrating Duluth's Sister Cities International's interrelationships and was passionately produced by Labovitz, under the auspices of the Tweed Museum of Art in collaboration with Duluth Sister Cities, International, and the University of Minnesota Duluth, School of Fine Arts.

Ken Bloom is the Director of the Tweed Museum of Art in Duluth, MN.

Inspired by Rania for Japan (detail), 2017
Acrylic on Tyvek®
415.5" by 30"
Anne Labovitz

"...Anne is the ultimate abstractionist. Unsurprisingly her color-field work is a contemporaneous and hugely related practice. Saturated with hues of pink, orange, purple, and turquoise, these compositions operate within several genres — one evoking the stained raw canvases of Helen Frankenthaler, the other alluding to the calligraphic marks of Cy Twombly with their mergers of line and script."

Darsie Alexander

Has anyone here seen Anne Labovitz?

Anne is waiting patiently for me at a lunch spot in Minneapolis, in a cool glass-enclosed restaurant overlooking the city streets. I'm at least twenty minutes late and first impressions are already out the window. Anne is looking very professional — hair pulled back, suit jacket, fashionable eyewear. She is smiling, nicely. She is very forgiving, poised even, and understanding of my busy schedule. Anne is good at the ice-breakers: Do I like Minneapolis so far? Kids? Job? Has my stuff arrived yet? I'm not sure when the lunch ended, but when it did I realized, to my horror, that I had done most of the talking. Very bad practice for a curator who works with artists — and Anne is an artist, first and foremost, and that was my introduction. I'm herewith attempting a redux, now at least ten years anon and many lunches (and a few cocktails) later.

For those who know Anne, who have met and experienced her, there is really very little one can do to untangle the person she is from the art that she creates. Her personality, desires, fears, relationships — it's all there. In hindsight, that first meeting was but a little sliver of all that space that Anne occupies, be it in her career, board roles, family life, student responsibilities, and countless other preoccupations that she writes, paints, acts and thinks about. People are the driving force of her life and the connector that shapes all through-lines of her art. Painted portraits — some alive with feeling, others seemingly expressionless — talk across the walls of Anne's brightly-lit studio. Their thoughts perform substrates of her compositions buried in layers of text, stories, and color. Friends, peers, and family members, all with their own narratives, are quite literally written into the work. Anne's painting is also a tale of her process, often over a period of many months, when according to the artist she aims to "fossilize, preserve and record each set of marks as a single event..." In so doing, she taps into her own memories and associations of the person she is depicting. These associations come by way of interviews she has conducted, photographs and other documentation kept on hand for reference to deepen the texture of the subject, often in visible ways. Mostly there is first-hand knowledge of the subject him-or-herself, gleaned in ways similar to our first encounter in the restaurant, the slow beginning of an accumulation of experience and personal connection that is the inspiration, and, in some ways, the responsibility of her art.

Responsibility is a strange term to use when talking about painting, but it goes back once again to the individual who is this artist and the civic place her work has always occupied. *122 Conversations* is the perfect example. Launched in 2012, the piece incorporates interviews conducted with ten residents of six global cities. Created over Skype, they take shape around basic human questions (name, occupation, etc) that anyone can answer, but that are also revealing of factors including age, background, and cultural context. These conversations then become the foundation of a traveling exhibition — sometimes of remarkably long and colorful works can be rolled and packed into lightweight carry-on luggage. Talking as a means of relaxing and getting to know a subject was a strategy Anne learned early on from her grandmother, also an artist. As a child, the older woman would distract Anne with a toy or trinket, using

Untitled 14 (Black), 2013
Woodcut print with speedball ink, acrylic, graphite, and pastel on primed canvas
48" by 36"
Anne Labovitz

the "sitting" as social time to connect with her grandchild while getting to the business of her art. When Anne herself became a mother in 1998, she also worked with kids doing class portraits, discovering once again that chatting can put people at ease. It can also add levity to a process that can be intimate and vulnerable (who doesn't feel awkward knowing they are being examined through the eyes of an artist?). She has said recently, "For many years, I did portraits as a way "into" someone — a way to connect, a way to see." And these moments of connection ultimately lend a compassion and humility to her work, allowing the deep crevices of hidden feeling and emotion to come forward through dense and imprecise surfaces that often resemble encrustations, suggesting the many layers that constitute our individual selves.

Giving material form to a psychological state or emotion is a daunting challenge for any artist, but it is nonetheless one that has occupied them for generations. The raw, gnarly that Anne has produced over the years (and one in particular, the riveting *Untitled 14 [Black]* with its off-register scratches and compressed field) bring to mind the early twentieth century experiments of Max Beckmann, Ernst Ludwig Kirchner, and Emile Nolde; for what it's worth, Anne has spent considerable time in Berlin with family and pursing graduate studies, where she has had first-hand access to these legendary members of Expressionism. Her reliefs share with these earlier figures an abiding interest in pathos and human frailty. In some of her works, a face is submerged in veils of thick black ink, alluding to feelings of despair and hopelessness in her work. Elsewhere, floating embers of light and shadow form auratic halos around the heads of children and girls in particular, suggesting an interest in the challenges facing young women today. Thoughtful interpretation and pure conjecture collide in these readings of her work, shaped as they are by a multitude of forces, be they personal, social, spiritual or fantastical.

Within this language of 'portraiture' (itself such a limited term), Anne is the ultimate abstractionist. Unsurprisingly her color-field work is a contemporaneous and hugely related practice. Saturated with hues of pink, orange, purple, and turquoise, these compositions operate within several genres — one evoking the stained raw canvases of Helen Frankenthaler, the other alluding to the calligraphic marks of Cy Twombly with their mergers of line and script. Sometimes a head is visible from behind the veils of marks and color. While no less inspired by specific experience (in some cases people, in others places) the compositions are singular and energetic. One senses nature in their loose swirls, soft horizons, and bursts color. Opting for exuberance over restraint, they exude pleasure and optimism. This was particularly important for the artist after the divisive 2016 election when dark/light metaphors pervaded her work. A sun is visible cutting through the haze of several 'color wash' works from this period, suggesting the potential to pierce the aqueous surface of her work with a new opening and possibility.

Reflecting on the work of a prolific artist — and Anne is certainly one — is a welcome opportunity for those of us involved in contemporary art, and we can be deft interpreters of lives and history. But any pretense to objectivity must be acknowledged as such when writing about one who is simultaneously an independent creative force and lasting friend. These two roles are inextricably bound in my appraisal of Anne and her work. It is difficult to muffle the sound of Anne's enthusiastic string of expletives when describing the *Fuck Triptych* painting (assuredly a tame mantle compared to the live performance), or to suppress the image of a colorful scarf once worn to an opening that resembles a painting of the same period. It's a vibrant cacophony. Like life. Like Anne.

Fuck Triptych, 2014
Acrylic with polymer emulsion on canvas
17" by 41" by 3" (Collection of Christian Sirek)
Anne Labovitz

Darsie Alexander is the Susan and Elihu Rose Chief Curator at the Jewish Museum. Previously she held curatorial positions at the Walker Art Center, Baltimore Museum of Art and The Museum of Modern Art, New York. Most recently she served as Executive Director of the Katonah Museum of Art in Westchester County, New York. Alexander has curated numerous exhibitions focusing on postwar American and European art, notably *International Pop* (2015-2016); *The Spectacular of Vernacular* (2011); *Franz West, To Build a House You Start with the Roof: Work, 1972-2008* (2008); and *SlideShow* (2005). She maintains an interest in interdisciplinary practice stemming from her work on the Merce Cunningham Dance Archive. Alexander has served on various boards and foundation panels. She is a graduate of Bates College and earned her graduate degree from Williams College.

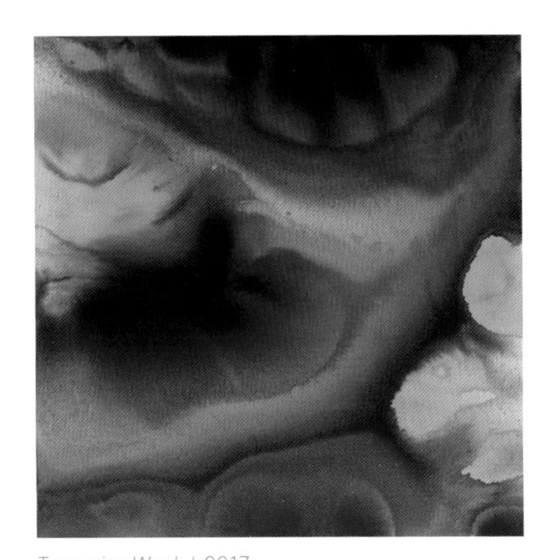

Turquoise Wash I, 2017
Acrylic on canvas
24" by 24" by 2"
Anne Labovitz

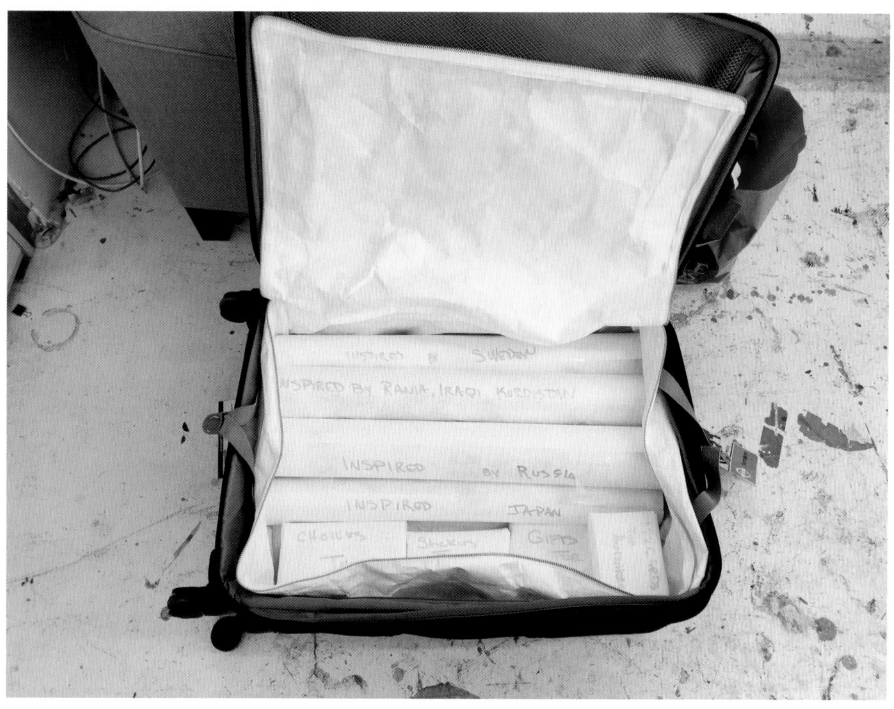

Black, rolling, suitcase packed with the entire site specific exhibition for Petrozavodsk, Russia, in the "Mary Poppins" white Tyvek® bag inside.

Participants in Thunder Bay, *All Sign Together*, contributing to the exhibit.

"With *122 Conversations*, Labovitz shifted her practice to include not only painting and mark making (with nods to traditional mediums and genres) but also to social practice, specifically the facilitation of shared authorship, dialogical processes, and sociopolitical gestures. In this work she allows — as well as encourages — her subjects to co-create elements of the exhibition."

Jack Becker

Creative Abundance

I've been very fortunate to work in the broad and expanding field of public art for more than forty years. I've learned that public art isn't an art form; it's a field of inquiry, like medicine or science. Artists of all stripes are experimenting and testing theories of cause and effect in the public sphere. They treat the city like it's their laboratory, a venue for all kinds of creative experimentation.

The project *122 Conversations: Person to Person, Art Beyond Borders* by Anne Labovitz is a new kind of experiment involving a six-venue, international touring exhibition; participatory interventions inside and outside the gallery; dialogues and discussions with more than 2,000 participants; documentation, video, and importantly, artworks sited within the public realm. Public art, as a practice, offers unlimited opportunities for collaboration, for ideas that shape our built and social environments, and efforts that influence change — locally and globally. Artists are no longer relegated to working in isolation or simply plopping personal expressions in public spaces. Today, artists can write their own job descriptions, follow their personal passions, and collaborate with anyone and everyone. From earthworks and wrapped buildings to bridge lighting and flash mob events, artists are redefining what public art can be every day.

Public art is evidence of our shared humanity. Over the past two decades, the field has evolved from art *in* public to art by, for, and about the public. It's less of a monologue and more of a dialogue. Public artists, in a sense, custom curate experiences for us. It's a kind of creative caring for daily life. Social practitioner Jen Reyes describes this type of work as "a lived practice."

This dialogical and situational practice is embodied in Labovitz's art. Her work is reflective of a creative, reciprocal relationship between herself as the artist, the physicality of the artwork, and the engagement of her audience/participants. She has learned to tap into and trust her intuition and let her insatiable curiosity tell her where to go, what to do, and how to navigate new territories. *122 Conversations* highlights Labovitz's many connections to place and conveys her urgency to visually manifest these connections. During one of several interviews I had with Labovitz, she told me, "My artist friend Harold Adams, who is 94, said if you have an idea in the studio you have to do it. Period.... It is like you are bound in a certain way to try it."

Working more publically and intuitively — without a roadmap or a compass — hasn't deterred Labovitz. In fact, it seems to be one of her key motivators. She has expanded her practice beyond painting, drawing, printmaking, experimental film, and participatory performance art. She's moved beyond exhibiting her works in galleries and museums and now considers public spaces as fair game. At the core of her work, however, is her fascination with people and the human experience.

New Approaches in Public Practice

With *122 Conversations: Person to Person, Art Beyond Borders*, Labovitz dives head first into the big world of public art and the field of socially engaged art. Working within these realms, she utilizes social practice methods such as dialogue, co-creation, and participatory actions, while also including quiet moments of reciprocal connection and gestures of generosity as part of her work. Text and dialogue are built up over time and through discussions with participants. In this way, her work is a very social, dialogical practice; the process is the art as much as the actual artwork. Yet, for Labovitz, the beauty of the final artwork is vital. "I think aesthetic is really important... beauty is primal," she explains. Indeed, the work is not just beautiful; it is seductively engaging.

In essence, Labovitz's work is about connections and visualizing dialogue. Her keen sense of observation and ability to relate to practically anyone has allowed her to put herself in a room of strangers from literally anywhere in the world. She puts everyone at ease, engages in conversation, joins in artmaking, and shares stories. Labovitz uses her art to build community and bridge divides. As with her portrait paintings, in which handwritten quotes drawn from her subjects are embedded, words play an integral role in her art — even if they aren't meant to be read in the traditional sense. Here, the words inform the art, and the art of conversation takes center stage as her primary medium. Feminist art history teaches us that dialogue can be a powerful method of engagement. Suzanne Lacy's *Whisper, the Waves, the Wind* (1983-1984) was a project where the artist worked with 154 older women in a public art intervention on the beaches in La Jolla, California. Sitting at white cloth-covered tables, they discussed their lives, their relationships, their hopes, and their fears. Similarly, Labovitz engaged in intense Skype dialogues with participants who discussed their lives and the common bonds they shared with others around the world. Recorded conversations were then played over and over again in her studio as Labovitz created the scroll paintings.

With *122 Conversations*, Labovitz shifted her practice to include not only painting and mark making (with nods to traditional mediums and genres), but also to social practice, specifically the facilitation of shared authorship, dialogical processes, and sociopolitical gestures. In this work she allows — as well as encourages — her subjects to co-create elements of the exhibition. Over the course of the project, her subjects/participants/viewers grew in number and in scale — from individuals, to communities, to cities, and in this case, a cohort of cities around the globe. This convergence reflects a shift in conventional thinking of public art practice — one that is both inside and outside the gallery space.

Thinking Globally, Acting Locally — Sister Cities

Many community-engaged artists and creatively minded activists embrace the idea of thinking globally and acting locally. Important and universal ideas are often investigated while local sociopolitical and historical contexts are negotiated. The *122 Conversations* project exemplifies this global/local notion. Labovitz grew up in Duluth, Minnesota, a place she refers to as "geographically isolated, with limited exposure to languages, cultures, and lifestyles different from my own." Her original idea was to travel an exhibition of her artworks to Duluth's Sister Cities, but she soon realized that "it must be about the inhabitants of each city for it to be relevant." She then approached Sister Cities and Tweed Museum of Art to be partners in a different kind of project — one that connected communities in evolving gestures of creative dialogue.

Duluth has a combined 122-year relationship with its five sister cities — Rania, Iraqi Kurdistan; Växjö, Sweden; Petrozavodsk, Russia; Thunder Bay, Canada; and Ohara-Isumi City, Japan — hence the title *122 Conversations*. Duluth's Sister Cities International seeks to promote peace through mutual respect, understanding, and cooperation — one individual, one community at a time. Their mission resonated with Labovitz, given her belief that art can be a catalyst for positive social change. "The act of making a genuine, heartfelt connection with a stranger is essential."

Labovitz embraces what many artists have historically undertaken — engaging in a creative, international exchange. Such mechanisms within art history include not only Sister City exchanges but also artists' residencies and U.S. government-sponsored cultural diplomacy exhibitions extending from the 1930s to today. Not surprisingly, Robert Rauschenberg's 1980s Rauschenberg Overseas Cultural Interchange (ROCI) project influenced Labovitz's project. Elsewhere in Minnesota, both Minneapolis and St. Paul have engaged in art exchanges with their respective Sister Cities going back as far as the 1980s. Indeed, since 1956, when President Eisenhower initiated the Sister Cities program, it has generated one of the most impactful, yet overlooked, cultural exchange initiatives in our country's history, and typically results in projects sited in public spaces.

Gift Giving as Art

The late Larry Harvey, visionary founder of Burning Man, an outrageously artful, temporary community that convenes annually in the Nevada desert, once gave a lecture at the Walker Art Center in Minneapolis. "In Bohemia," he declared, "in the natural world of the artist, there exists an economy of creative abundance, because this is a world of gift giving. At the same time, we've taken the playfulness of art and defined it in terms of social utility. We've always encouraged forms of art that convene society around themselves… A more potent organizer of human communities is hard to imagine."

Labovitz's practice embodies the idea of creative abundance. She is intensely interested in the notion of a reciprocal exchange — visually, emotionally, and psychologically. She also always includes a type of take-away, or what she considers a gift, for participants and often viewers of her work. Like the artist Félix González-Torres, who would invite viewers to take away with them a piece of paper or a small hard candy as part of his exhibitions, Labovitz is interested in creative exchange as well as generosity.

Again, similar to González-Torres, she's also interested in artworks that embody relationships. Following her extended online Skype conversations with ten individuals from each Sister City, Labovitz strived to interpret her engagement experiences and created artworks as gifts to each individual as well as each community in return for their time and their stories. "When I made these paintings — in my heart, in my mind, or in my body — each piece was conceived as a gift to that city. I am bringing something that is like a hello or a welcome to a friendship, and it should feel that way. That is important to me. So that's how I created them, knowing I had to remain true to those interviews. I listened to them more than a dozen times each and ruminated over them. I love those interviews because I would listen and write what they said over and over. And it's because there was this spiritual moment where people shared themselves in a beautiful way. They really wanted to be a part of something, and that tells me people want to — *we want to* — be together, you know, as human beings. Without exception, people were so eager and wanted to be involved and participate and share, and it's moving. So, for me I felt like I owed them something." This urgent need took the form of "gratitude paintings" and *Certificates of Participation*.

Lewis Hyde, in his book *The Gift: Creativity and the Artist in the Modern World*, states: "A work of art is a gift, not a commodity. Or, to state the modern case with more precision, that works of art exist simultaneously in two 'economies,' a market economy and a gift economy. Only one of these is essential, however: a work of art can survive without the market, but where there is no gift there is no art." For artists working in the public art field, the notion of giving back or gifting is quite familiar. After all, we don't think of public art as something that's for sale; it's freely accessible to everyone. There's no price tag on a work of public art. And, to a great extent, public artists value working in communities as a way to *make a difference* in the world, rather than make a profit. With *122 Conversations*, Labovitz clearly taps into the gift economy and a currency of kindness. There's a cause and effect phenomenon involved with offering a gift, inviting strangers to take part in a public art project, or facilitating a group activity. It invites reciprocation and inspires participants to further share with others, thus generating an energy that multiplies exponentially.

Like González-Torres, Labovitz uses malleable variations of installations, meaning there can be multiple ways the exhibition can be set up. These public interventions — some more public than others — were site-specific, intended to respond to contextual considerations. In response to each of *122 Conversations*' six venues, each exhibition was different and responded empathetically to each place — in relation to people, the space, and logistics. For example, in Iraqi Kurdistan and Russia, a volunteer courier brought the work. In a way, the specificity of each installation was also a gift — one that is created especially for that place.

The notion of multiples in Labovitz's work — for example many pieces were sent in suitcases — recalls poignant works from the Fluxus movement, a forerunner to social practice, and González-Torres' method of art making. These are traveling gifts that facilitate connection. Labovitz explains, "I document human connection, dialogue, and relationships, always considering the notion of temporality." In public practice, community engagement and conversations are an important currency. The "artworks" are more often evidence of the process, documentation, recordings, transcriptions, and translations. In this way, the artwork goes beyond time and space or place to a site of healing.

Conversation as a Process for Healing

Through her interviewing process, and the labor-intensive artmaking that followed, Labovitz sought to discover common ground and share her discovery as a means of healing, bridging divide, and forging new alliances. Supported by overwhelming evidence that the arts contribute to individual and community well-being, *122 Conversations* ambitiously posits that this can happen on a global scale.

I find Labovitz's methodology compelling and refreshing, allowing each successive engagement and the people who participated to inform the artmaking and the planning for the next engagement, a kind of iterative, improvisational, gestural style. The artist allowed each situation to inform the creativity she would apply. "In a certain way," she said "you have to be agile in your thinking and your process.... As an artist, you can't control what is going to happen. Even losing the work. For example, when it went to Iraq, I thought it will either come back or it won't. It will be part of the story no matter what."

Community engagement as process was embedded in Labovitz's *122 Conversations*. The work made up of markings, words, handwritten transcriptions of interviews in their native language — all packaged to fit neatly within a specially designed suitcase for traveling (complete with instructions). She developed aprons for use at the artmaking workshops, allowing each host community to get fully engaged, participate actively in the project — kids got to interview each other, for example — make their own art, wear the art, and carry small squares, or tiles, of their art with them, dispersing the project in unexpected and sometimes surprising ways. Labovitz explains: "I interviewed a person from Iraqi Kurdistan who spoke about bringing a friend of his with him in his pocket, and how important that was for him because that's how they could be together because they were separated, by war... so it's like having people in the pockets [of the aprons], and I just love that....

"In places like Kurdistan, where I knew there was strife and people were fighting for their lives, I felt compelled to show people that someone cared, like you're belonging to something, with intention and friendship and love," Labovitz explains. "So, I just poured everything into it, and when the suitcase was opened, there was this *whoosh* of color and it felt alive."

There was an evolution to *122 Conversations*, from Labovitz's first trip to the last; modifications, adjustments, and improvements were made along the way. There was a mix of scale, from intimate tile making to the large hanging banners displayed in public spaces. The banners, likewise, grew in scale. By the time the project got to Japan, the banners were 35 feet long, offering a dramatic enhancement to a public building.

As with most community-oriented art practices, artists continually reflect on process, engagement, and the manifestation of their work. In addition to all the conversations Labovitz has had with others, she was openly having a conversation with herself. "In a sense, you are holding up a mirror so that you are allowing yourself to see what you are doing through other people's eyes — through their own lenses, through their own values, through their own issues they're dealing with in their community."

Labovitz is an artist who likes to throw herself into new situations. She embraces the unknown as an opportunity for rethinking and renewing. With *122 Conversations*, she taps into the global interest of participatory culture. People don't want to passively witness art; they want to actively participate in it. They want to help create art or interact with it. This inclination may be a reaction to today's isolating technology, but more so, I believe, it's people's desire to connect with each other on a more human, authentic, or personal level. Artists like Labovitz are making a difference in the world with their creativity. This difference-making only comes about once the artist taps into their own humanity. "I need to be together with myself, my art, and with people because I have gifts as a human. I love to make people feel good, so why wouldn't I use that in my own practice? ... The world is pretty small," says Labovitz, in hindsight.

This is the kind of thinking that sustains me today. I would argue that, with artists like Anne Labovitz, the world will grow even smaller, and the bonds that connect us will overpower any differences that divide us.

Jack Becker founded Forecast Public Art in 1978, and now serves as director of Forecast's Creative Services program. As a public artist, administrator, and veteran consultant, Jack specializes in developing projects and plans for communities large and small. He especially enjoys projects that connect the ideas and energies of artists with the needs and opportunities of communities. He has organized more than 70 exhibitions, 50 publications, and numerous special events. Becker received a Bachelor of Fine Arts (BFA) degree from the Minneapolis College of Art and Design, studying under such artists as Siah Armajani, Kinji Akagawa and Andrew Leicester. Born in St. Louis, Missouri, he also studied there at Washington University and Webster University, as well as the Croydon College of Art and Design in Great Britain. Widely acknowledged as a leader in the field, Jack is the founding publisher of Public Art Review. In 2007, he received the Public Art Network Award of Excellence from Americans for the Arts, and, in 2014, he received a lifetime achievement award from the College Art Association, through their Public Art Dialogue program.

Mayor of Rania, Iraqi Kurdistan, Ali Hammad Bagg with grandson during Skype interview, January 2015

"Anne was able to bring people together, give them a place to be heard, give them a break from their realities, and allow them to be part of a global project that intended to show us that no matter where we come from or how different we may seem, there is a common essence in all of us..."

Omayra Alvarado

Who said everything is lost I come to offer my heart[1]

To talk about *122 Conversations* we need to talk about hope, kindness, and care; we need to think about what art can do for the world we are living in right now. In these convoluted times, filled with hate and fear for what seems foreign or strange, where the color of our skin, our gender, our sexual preferences or our nationality still divides us; a world where we ignore the pain of others just because we don't want to be bothered; where the value of a person has been reduced to its ability to produce and consume — to serve a system that sees us as data to analyze consumerism trends — in a world like this, we need artists that can step out of their comfort zone and take risks within their own practices and question the role of art in our society. Anne Labovitz has done this in such a subtle and dedicated way in this long-term project, giving us the opportunity to remind ourselves that just the simple act of listening to each other can be a powerful tool towards building a better society.

In materialistic and cold times, the act of caring for the other and for oneself is an act of resistance. Labovitz's *122 Conversations* became a way to circumvent and defy a self-centered system; a way to establish an economy that was not related to a monetary exchange of resources, but instead, was based on the desire to hear and to get to know the other — providing an emotional connection, establishing an economy of friendship.

For over five years Labovitz immersed herself in a multidisciplinary exploration that included interviews, exhibitions, public interaction, and educational workshops that explored how a political, social, and cultural platform can be turned into an act of care. Inspired by the mission of the Sister Cities International, (a program that seeks to promote peace through mutual respect, understanding, and cooperation — one individual, one community at a time) Labovitz conducted sixty interviews in six different countries — that are the focus of this essay — using a standard series of questions like "What is your name? What is your favorite color? How old are you?" Anne was able to bring people together, give them a place to be heard, give them a break from their realities, and allow them to be part of a global project that intended to show us that no matter where we come from or how different we may seem, there is a common essence in all of us; an essence that goes beyond morals, and instead appeals to a more poetic and honest necessity, our own urgency to live.

This long-term collaboration embodied Labovitz's own personal interest in exploring human interactions and the necessity to see *the other*, to recognize the basic feelings that unite as human beings. Hence this exchange between artist and subject transcended conversation and became gestures of generosity, friendship, reciprocity, and a path for community building and emotional exchange.

In *122 Conversations*, the artist's presence and interaction with her interviewees reveals the power of a conscious body, the tensions that are generated by a body that is in control of its emotions and has stepped into a vulnerable state, opening a door for those around it. This door takes the viewer (in this case the interviewee) to a place in their mental and emotional body that will let them feel free to be vulnerable and honest. This state could

Note:

1. "Yo vengo a ofrecer mi corazón / I come to offer my heart" is a song by Argentinian musician Fito Páez published in 1985.

Labovitz interviewing Japan Sister City Deputy Mayor Koichi Uezima and translator, at historic Glensheen Manor in Duluth at Fourth Fest, 2015

Video still, *122 Conversations* introductory video. 60 seconds. Created by Matt Dressel with stills and video by Anne Labovitz, 2015.

be understood as a poetic instant[2], where two apparent opposites meet and connect in such a profound way that their differences are erased. The intention and repetition of this act has infused this project with such strength that when you listen to these interviews, you can't help but to be lured into this instant as well.

There is another aspect of this project that is important to talk about and that is the relationship between personal and political, between the ideas that create a *political self* and an *intimate self* and how these two are bound by vulnerability and intimacy and how the connection between these concepts can strengthen the way we interact with others. Labovitz's project became a bridge for these two *selves* to encounter, and as Carol Hanisch stated in her essay *My Personal is Political*, "...personal problems are political problems. There are no personal solutions at this time. There is only collective action for a collective solution,"[3] there is a critical necessity to bring the notion of emotions and humanity not only into the political discussion but into the theoretical discourse of art as well.

Who said every thing is lost... I'll give you everything, and you'll give me something, Something that relieves me a little more. When there is no one near or far, I come to offer my heart.

Omayra Alvarado is a curator and gallerist from Bogotá, Colombia. She is one of the founders and executive director of Instituto de Visión, a gallery focusing on Latin-American artists with an international scope.

Notes:

2. Gaston Bachellard. "Poetic Instant and Metaphysical Instant," in *Intuition of the Instant*, trans. Eileen Rizo-Patron, Evanston, IL: Northwestern University Press, 2013.

3. Carol Hanisch. "The Personal Is Political". http://www.carolhanisch.org/CHwritings/PIP.html 1969

Gratitude Certificate of Participation, Thunder Bay, 2015
Acrylic on paper
30" by 44"
Anne Labovitz

Thunder Bay, Ontario, Canada

Inspired by Petrozavodsk for Canada, 2015
Acrylic, polymer emulsion, and Caran d'Ache with graphite on Rives BFK paper
40" by 40"
Anne Labovitz

Inspired by Rania for Canada, 2015
Acrylic, polymer emulsion, and Caran d'Ache with graphite on Rives BFK paper
40" by 40"
Anne Labovitz

Inspired by Thunder Bay for Canada, 2015
Acrylic, polymer emulsion, and Caran d'Ache with graphite on Rives BFK paper
40" by 40"
Anne Labovitz

Inspired by Växjö for Canada, 2015
Acrylic, polymer emulsion, and Caran d'Ache with graphite on Rives BFK paper
40" by 40"
Anne Labovitz

Inspired by Petrozavodsk for Canada (detail), 2015
Acrylic, polymer emulsion, and Caran d'Ache with graphite on Rives BFK paper
40" by 40"
Anne Labovitz

Inspired by Ohara Isumi-City for Canada, 2015
Acrylic, polymer emulsion, and Caran d'Ache with graphite on Rives BFK paper
40" by 40"
Anne Labovitz

Inspired by Duluth for Canada, 2015
Acrylic, polymer emulsion, and Caran d'Ache with graphite on Rives BFK paper
40" by 40"
Anne Labovitz

Thunder Bay Art Gallery, installation, 2015

All Sign Together (Book), 2015
Acrylic, polymer emulsion, and Caran D'Ache with graphite on Rives BFK paper
40" by 40" by 5.5"
Anne Labovitz Citizens of Duluth, USA, Ohara Isumi-City, Japan, Thunder Bay, Canada, Rania, Iraqi Kurdistan, Petrozavodsk Russia, and Växjö, Sweden

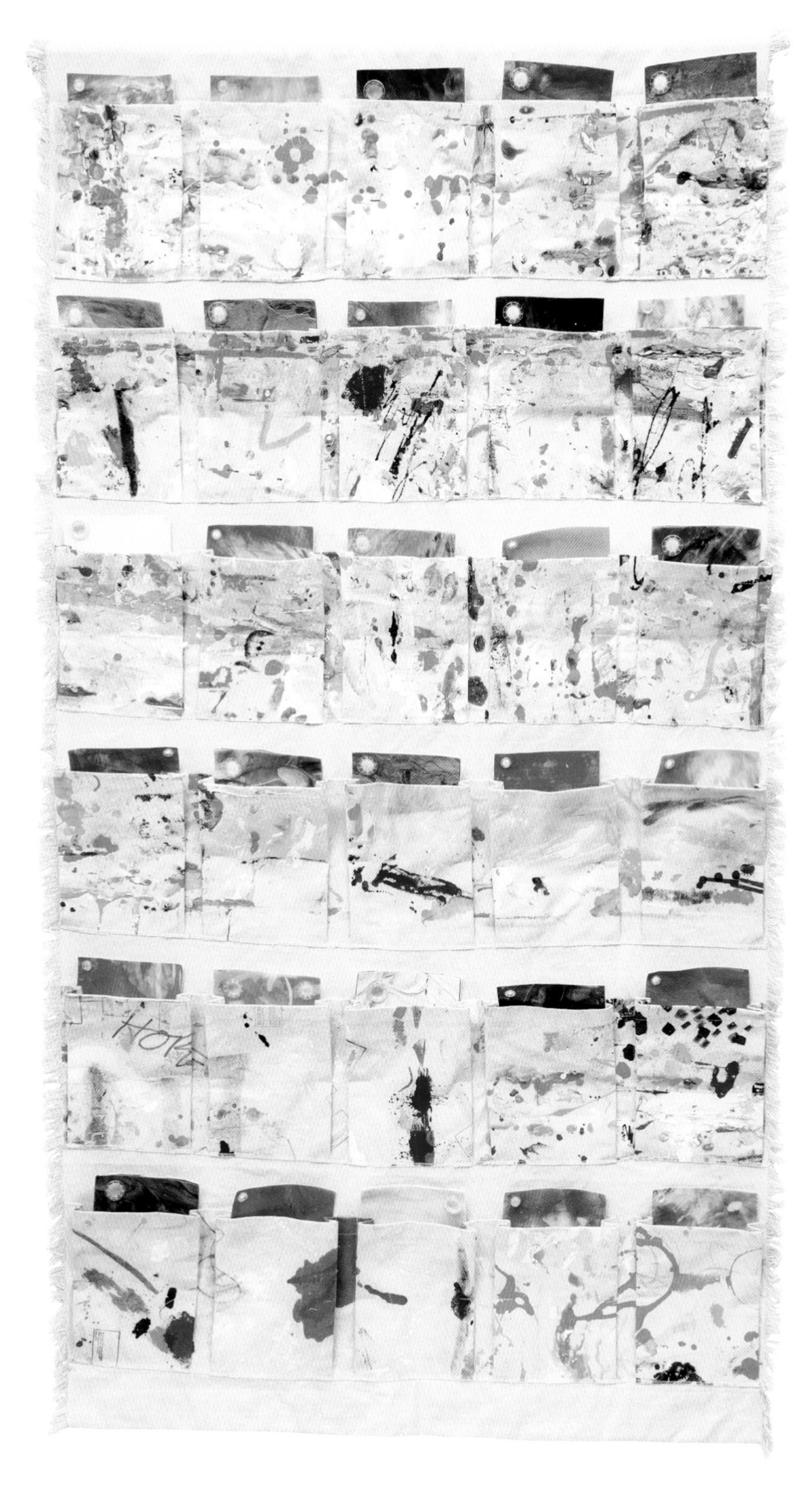

Choices Canvas Pockets, 2015
Collected studio drippings with thread on canvas pockets, 2015
75" by 41"
Anne Labovitz with Suy Path

Page 34/35
Choices Tiles, Thunder Bay, Canada, 2015
Acrylic and polymer emulsion on Rives BFK
6" x 6" each
Anne Labovitz with Citizens of Thunder Bay

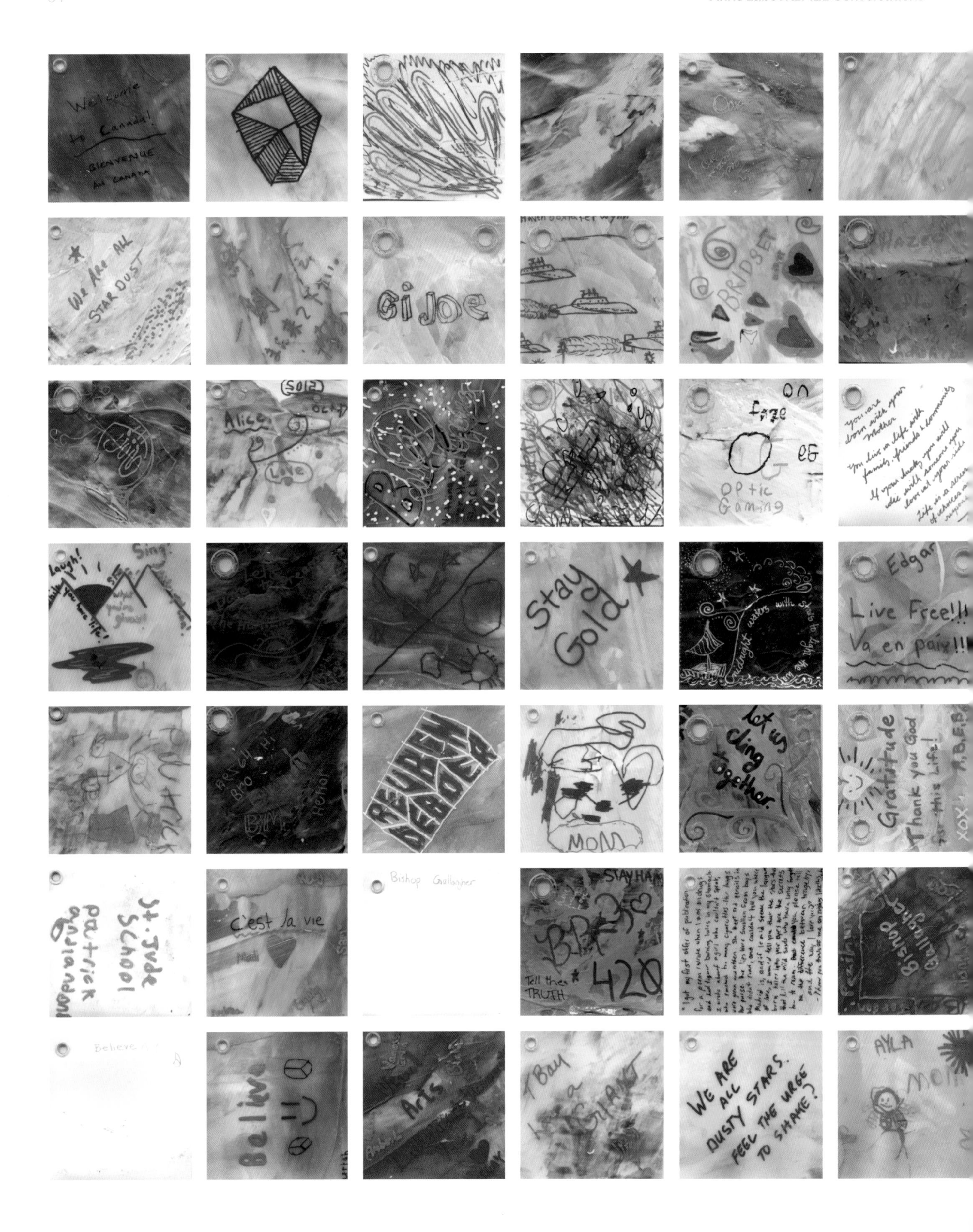
Welcome to Canada!
BIENVENUE AU CANADA
We Are All STAR DUST
Gi Joe
BRIDGET
Alice
Love
faze
Optic Gaming
Stay Gold
Edgar
Live Free!!!
Va en paix!!
REUBEN DEBOER
MOM
let us cling together.
Gratitude
Thank you God for this Life!
St. Jude School
C'est la vie
Bishop Gallagher
Tell the TRUTH
420
Believe
Arts
WE ARE ALL DUSTY STARS. FEEL THE URGE TO SHAKE?
AYLA

Someone told me
We are born alone
We live alone
and we die alone
What happens inbetween is up to you and you alone.
TRUE or FALSE ?
Assassins Creed
Breathe
MAX
It's good to see another perspective there's room for all ideas
ALL MY FAVORITE COLOURS IN ONE PLACE
WONDERFUL!
Don't FEAR THE BLACK CAT... Embrace him
Everyone's Beautiful and amazing and creative never let anyone let you Down
from East to West
through forests of tall tall trees through orchards and through mountains she traveled until she could smell the salt from the Sea
Live for what you Create, and die Protecting it.
- Gaga
@blakevans13
morgan.
"you made a Rebel of a careless man's careful daughter."
Our Lady of Charity school
all you need is
Just be Your self

Labovitz with students working on *All Sign Together*, Thunder Bay, 2015

Top (left): Interviewee Elle-Andra Warner at opening in Thunder Bay, 2015

Top (right): Public participation Thunder Bay, 2015

Middle (left): Public participation Thunder Bay, 2015

Middle (right): Thunder Bay interviewees Eleanor Albanese, Damon Dowbak, Michelle Dorosier, Labovitz, Elliott Doxtater-Wynn attending the opening of *122 Conversations* at Thunder Bay Art Gallery

Bottom (left): *Choices* artist book, Anne Labovitz and citizens of Thunder Bay

Bottom (right): Hanna Smith interviewee, 2015, Thunder Bay

Top (left): Student with *122 Conversations* gratitude stickers

Top (middle): Elliott Doxtater-Wynn during interview, 2015, Thunder Bay

Top (right): Student

Middle (left): Mr. and Mrs. Gary Cooper with Labovitz

Middle (right): Michelle Dorosier

Bottom: Opening celebration in Thunder Bay, 2015

Field Notes: Thunder Bay, Ontario, Canada

September 10 – October 19, 2015, at Thunder Bay Art Gallery

Context

Two years after initial project discussions began, the first exhibition for *122 Conversations* occurred in Thunder Bay, Ontario, Canada. Initially convincing people about the potential for this project was a challenge that pushed me to express myself more articulately and to develop strong core elements that would encompass the proposal. Sharon Godwin, Director Thunder Bay Art Gallery, said, *"When we were first approached about 18 months ago about the* 122 Conversations *project, we were a bit overwhelmed with the complexity of the endeavor. It felt very elaborate and ambitious. But then we met Anne Labovitz and we knew almost immediately that it would be possible. (Those of you who know Anne will understand!)".*

Process/Observations

A highlight of the Thunder Bay program that became an important central tenet of the project was the invitation to work with at-risk youth. Believing that positive change in the world can be accomplished one individual at a time, I chose to work with youth to draw out and identify poignant connections between us. I interviewed each participant face-to-face to create a platform for art as social expression. For Canada, the artworks were created with heavy acrylic and polymer emulsion and had a different form than the scrolls created for later venues. Initially, I conceived of the artworks as a type of multiple (Beuysian) or interchangeable sets. The four-square units of each set were envisioned as potentially intermixed according to the interests of the touring venues' preferences. This process wouldn't work when traveling the show — I had to change the material. During the exhibition, more than 600 participants created tiles that accompanied the show. The experience was exhilarating. I knew the tiles would be a fantastic connector.

Reflections/Insight

Artists face conceptual and physical challenges in the making of a body of work. We regularly develop work out of necessity or in response to a set of logistical problems. The Thunder Bay show revealed problems that would impact the touring plan. I knew the works had to be lighter for transport. Notably, it was important that the art not be cumbersome for willing volunteers to carry. This meant not only shifts in size, medium, and material were necessary, but the paintings needed a new surface. From this point onward, the form of the work was transformed into Tyvek® scrolls. It took four months of experimentation to master and develop effective techniques to work on this unorthodox material.

Learning about the sociopolitical and historical nuances that affect the people and places I've encountered reaches to the core of my artistic practice — social engagement with emphasis on being open to differences. A striking aspect of my relationships with people in Thunder Bay was the influence shared with me by First Nation artists, filmmakers, and writers. It was an honor to work with Sharon and others at the First Nations Gallery in Thunder Bay (Northwestern Ontario's primary art gallery specializing in the work of contemporary First Nations artists). I am grateful for these experiences.

Participants

Rick Lang, Damon Dowbak, Eleanor Albanese, Elliott Doxtater-Wynn, Keith Hobbs, Michelle Dorosier, Gary Cooper, Lauryn Eady, Hannah Smith, and Elle-Andra Warner.

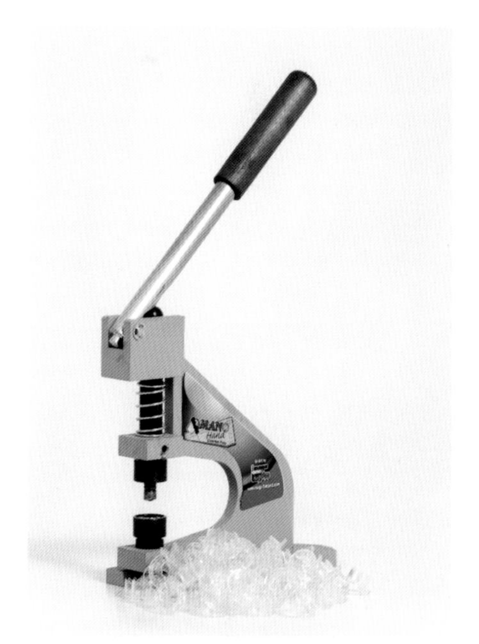

The Grommet machine used to prepare all the works for hanging

Gratitude Certificate of Participation, Rania, 2015
Acrylic on Rives BFK paper
30" by 44"
Anne Labovitz

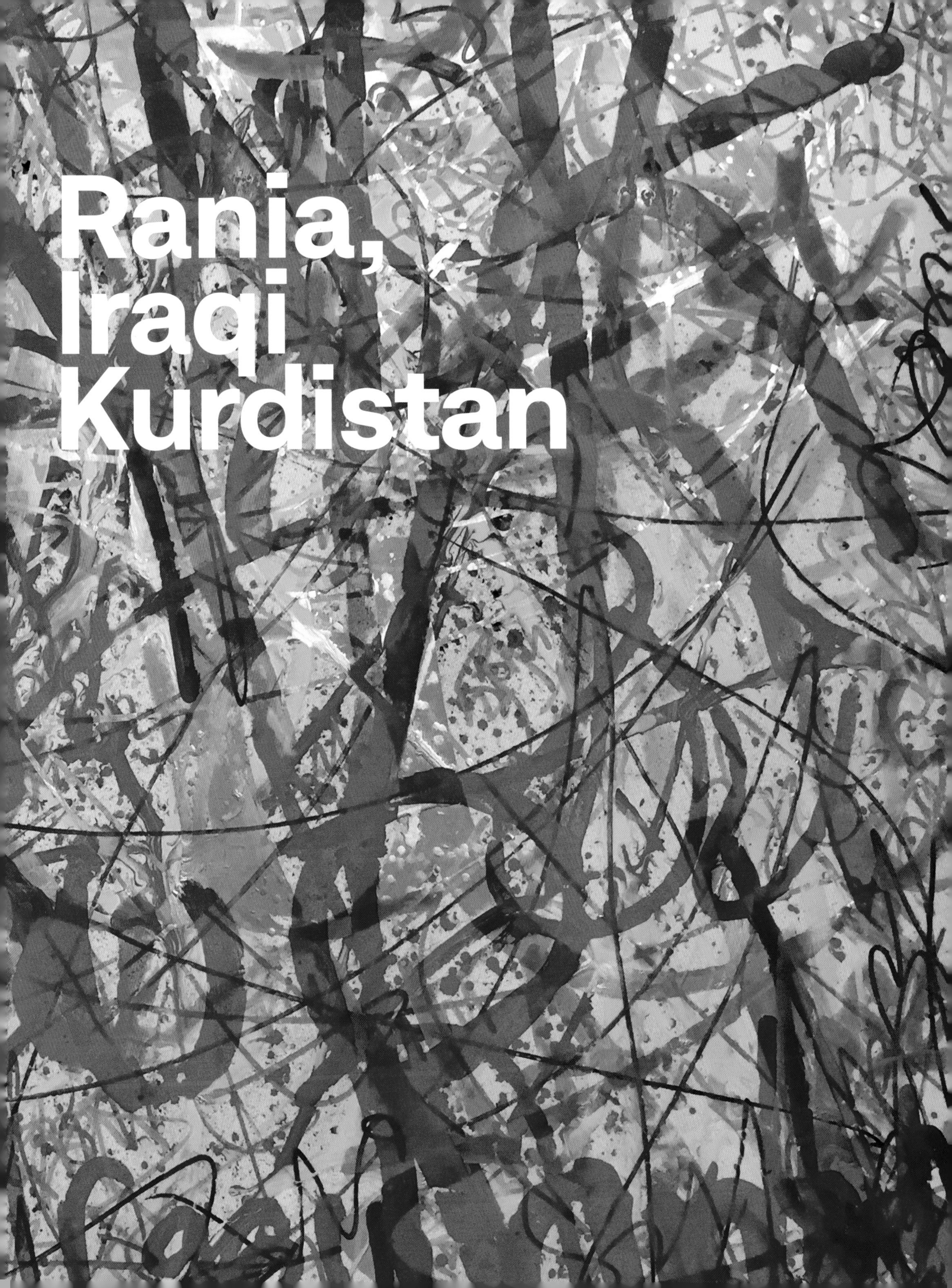
Rania,
Iraqi
Kurdistan

Inspired by Duluth for Iraqi Kurdistan, 2016
Acrylic on Tyvek®
Diptych 98" by 24" (left), 102.25" by 24" (right)
Anne Labovitz
(left scroll permanent collection in Rania, Iraqi Kurdistan)

Inspired by Ohara Isumi-City for Iraqi Kurdistan, 2016
Acrylic on Tyvek®
Diptych 74.5" by 24" (left), 75.25" by 24" (right)
Anne Labovitz

Inspired by Petrozavodsk for Iraqi Kurdistan, 2016
Acrylic on Tyvek®
Diptych 116.5" by 24" (left), 102.75" by 24" (right)
Anne Labovitz

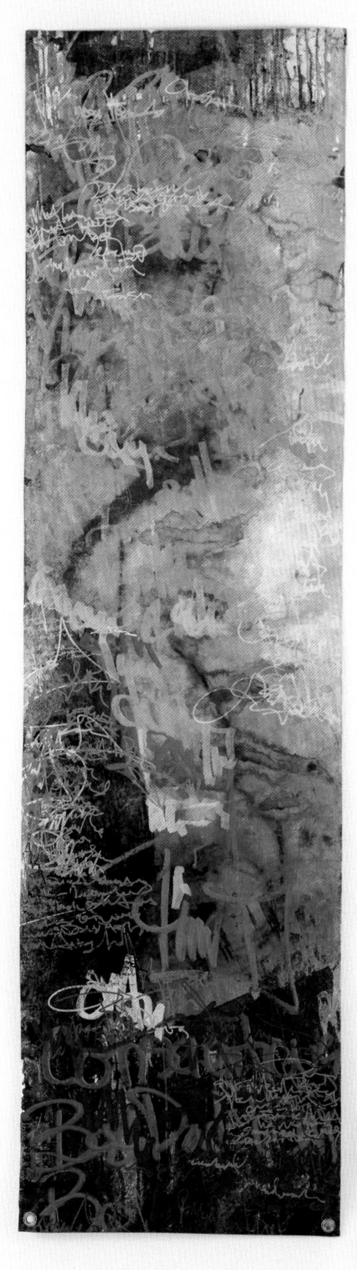

Inspired by Rania for Iraqi Kurdistan, 2016
Acrylic on Tyvek®
Diptych 80" by 24" (left), 133.5" by 24" (right)
Anne Labovitz
(left scroll permanent collection in Rania, Iraqi Kurdistan)

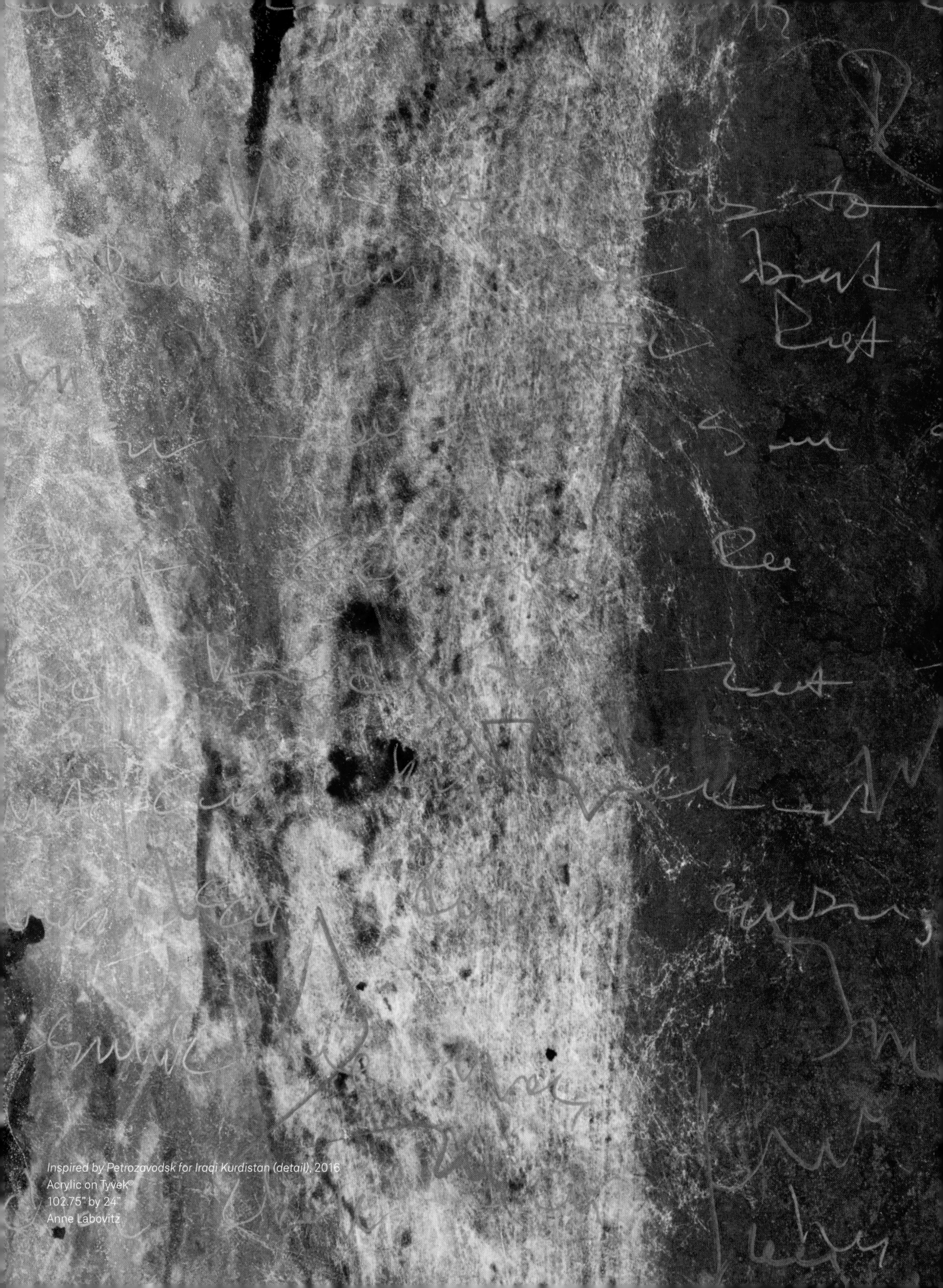

Inspired by Petrozavodsk for Iraqi Kurdistan (detail), 2016
Acrylic on Tyvek®
102.75" by 24"
Anne Labovitz

Inspired by Thunder Bay for Iraqi Kurdistan, 2016
Acrylic on Tyvek®
Diptych 112.5" by 24" (left), 139.75" by 24" (right)
Anne Labovitz

Inspired by Växjö for Iraqi Kurdistan, 2016
Acrylic on Tyvek®
Diptych 107" by 24" (left), 134.25" by 24" (right)
Anne Labovitz

University of Raparin, installation, 2017

Sun Scroll/United Under the Night Sky, Rania, 2017
Acrylic on Tyvek®
158" by 24" (left), 148.75" by 24" (right)
Anne Labovitz

Large Choices Apron, Rania (2), 2017
Stickers on Tyvek® with thread
51" by 45"
Anne Labovitz with Suy Path and Citizens of Thunder Bay

Page 54/55
Choices Tiles, Rania, 2017
Acrylic on Tyvek®
5" by 7" each
Anne Labovitz with Citizens of Rania

I'm 17 year old
I love Ranya
I hope meet you in my Country and in my Business
I love
I love you
Ranya
Be kind to yourself & others
Gona
Mahamad
I Love you Ranya
I Love you Ranya
To the sister we love you Ranya
HELLO
MAN RAZ. ALMNEA.
Love
Happe
LANE
I wish pea
for Kurdis

SINA
MARWA
I LOVE
you
Ranya
Stronger friends
Brighter future
All the best to
people of Rania
and Duluth
I LOVE kurdstan
my nims: chalia
Hallo
LOVE
Happe
Be kind
to yourself
Hallo HALAP
Kurdstan
Salar
Lamka
Hope peace for
world
Shalia
12 years old
I love London

Choices, Rania, 2017

Top (left): Volunteer translating the banners, Rania

Top (right): *Choices*, Rania, 2017, Teacher with first grade students writing love notes to Duluth

Middle (left): Duluth Sister City delegate Gale Kerns presenting gift to Mayor Hiroshi Ota.

Middle (right): Placing color tiles onto window

Bottom: Ribbon cutting with former mayor and interviewee at Rania opening, 2017

Top (left): Student group in Rania exhibition

Top (right): Skype interview, 2015 with translator Khalid Qader and Rania participant Kurdo Aziz Bag

Middle (left): Student participation in Rania

Middle (right): Student group in Rania exhibition

Bottom: Michele Naar-Obed describing *122 Conversations* at the opening in Rania

Field Notes: Rania, Iraqi Kurdistan

January 16 – March 31, 2017 at the University of Raparin

Context

Two years after the initial Skype interviews between myself and Sister City friends in Rania, the second venue on the *122 Conversations* exhibition tour took place in Iraqi Kurdistan, at the University of Raparin. More than 100 people visited the exhibition, including an entire class of 2nd-grade students. I received the following note from Rania from Duluth DSCI delegate Koresh Lakhan: "*'Wow! Wow! This is hyper modern art at its best!', declared the Director of the Art Department here, as he stood there transfixed. I had to Google to find the definition of hyper modern, because this term was not in my vocabulary. He said the script (writings) on the banners were like musical notes, and a feast to the eyes. That same evening we had the grand opening, which drew a standing roomful of citizens from toddlers to senior citizens.*"

Process/Observations

At this point in the project it became evident that delivering an exhibit for Rania would be complicated by the political conflicts of the region. Having started working with the lightweight Tyvek®, I also began to think creatively about how to package the work. I decided to send the work in a white Tyvek® bag inside a basic, black rolling suitcase. Not a new idea, I was inspired by artists who have used one in their art. In my mind, a suitcase serves both as a metaphor and for literal transportation. I recall Marcel Duchamp's *Boite-en-Valise* (1948), which contained 70 or so of his artworks, as a well-known example. I was also inspired by Palestinian artist Mona Hatoum, who created *Traffic* in 2002, which referenced complex themes of exile and dislocation. With the suitcase I felt the work for *122 Conversations* would be conceptually and physically nuanced.

Reflections/Insight

Sadly, I was unable to travel to Kurdistan to interact with the people of Rania. Fortunately, my friend and peace activist Michele Naar-Obed carried the artwork and went further to organize the interviews for the project. This kindness was an invaluable service.

Another significance represented by suitcase travel is trust, a trust surpassed only by my gratitude for the care and attention paid to the artwork and installation by my Sister City colleagues in Rania. The Duluth Sister Cities official delegation that traveled to Rania included Jill and Koresh Lakhan, Jeri and Gale Kerns, and Michele Naar-Obed. The delegates assisted with hanging the show and facilitating public participation. The Rania leg of the journey was organized through the Rayal Center For Cultural Exchange.

Participants

Kurdo Aziz Bagg, Rubar Yousef, Mulla Abdulla Wasman Adam, Salah Ali Wais, Niazy Hama Aziz, Khalil Ali Abdulla, Salah Jamal Khurshid, Faruq Mala Fatih, Nigar Mohammed Ali, Ali Hammad Ali, and Ali Hammad Bagg.

Student groups, Rania, 2015

Young artist, Rania, *All Sign Together*

Gratitude Certificate of Participation, Växjö, 2015
Acrylic on Rives BFK paper
30' by 44"
Anne Labovitz

Växjö,
Sweden

Inspired by Duluth for Sweden, 2017
Acrylic on Tyvek®
Diptych 223" by 24" (left), 165" by 24" (right)
Anne Labovitz

Inspired by Ohara Isumi-City for Sweden, 2017
Acrylic on Tyvek®
Diptych 170.75" by 24" (left), 168" by 24" (right)
Anne Labovitz

Inspired by Petrozavodsk for Sweden, 2017
Acrylic on Tyvek®
Diptych 151" by 24" (left), 167.5" by 24" (right)
Anne Labovitz

Inspired by Rania for Sweden, 2017
Acrylic on Tyvek®
Diptych 149.75" by 24" (left), 159" by 24" (right)
Anne Labovitz

Choices, Växjö, 2017

122
Conversations
Interview Questions
122
Fall 7 times Get up
VEGAN FOR THE VOICELESS
Love is Crazy
LOVE
HEROES
TAGGA GÄRNA!

Inspired by Thunder Bay for Sweden, 2017
Acrylic on Tyvek®
Diptych 179" by 24" (left), 205" by 24" (right)
Anne Labovitz

Inspired by Växjö for Sweden, 2017
Acrylic on Tyvek®
Diptych 215" by 24" (left), 218" by 24" (right)
Anne Labovitz
(permanent collection City of Växjö)

Växjö Konsthall, installation, 2017

United Under the Night Sky, Växjö, 2017
Acrylic on Tyvek®
Diptych 308" by 24" (left), 227" by 24" (right)
Anne Labovitz

Large Choices Apron, Växjö (1), 2017
Stickers on Tyvek® with thread
50" by 44.5"
Anne Labovitz with Suy Path and Citizens of Thunder Bay and Rania

Page 74/75:
Choices Tiles, Växjö, 2017
Acrylic on Tyvek®
6" by 6" each
Anne Labovitz with Citizens of Växjö

I feel like I'm missing
something in my life bu
I'm not sure if its a
place, a person or just
a burrito
Have a nice day!
My name is Annika
I found friends for life
in Duluth
I am John
I Live with Chelly.
I am a teacher
I like to ride my
Bike
Tjetjenien!!!
Seni
Seviyorum!
With Love
Hello
it's me
I Love
you
Hej
Jag är
Regina Sahak
Jag är bra
LOVE
you
are
beuti
PATIENCE
AND
PASSION
Allstar
IS
HEROES
Signe
You are beutiful
Love is best
USA
Canada
Japan
LOVE
Sweden
Russia
Irak
I hope you have a good
LIFE!
World Freedom
Hello
RUSSia
Kasper
INTEGRITET
LOVE
Привет Россия!
Я надеюсь что
у вас всё хорош

FLUX.
FREDRIK
VILDA.DAH
VEKSJO
SVEDSKA
Du är Snäl
G.Stein
EVERYTHING IS A CIRCLE
Tremendous
"smooth"
352
Life's short
DON'T
make it shorter
LOVE
AYDAH
I Love you
DREAM Big
Love more
Love
TOGETHER
Hello Russia!
Music
HLR
Love you
Believe
Hope
Love
believe in yourself,
W.W.J.D
Never give up in Life
AYDAH
A M
#Växjö lakers
Smile
我爱你
Live
Learn
Laugh
You are beautiful,
don't let others
state otherwise
No Race
No gender
No class
No differences
No language
No Religion
Animals will have it better

Choices, Växjö, 2017
Växjö student wrote on her tile: “Hi! I hope you have your dream life. You must care of your life. You must laugh and have fun. Love too. #liveyourlife”

Bottom (left): Skype interview with Växjö participants

All others: Student groups in *Choices* and *All Sign Together*, Växjö, 2017

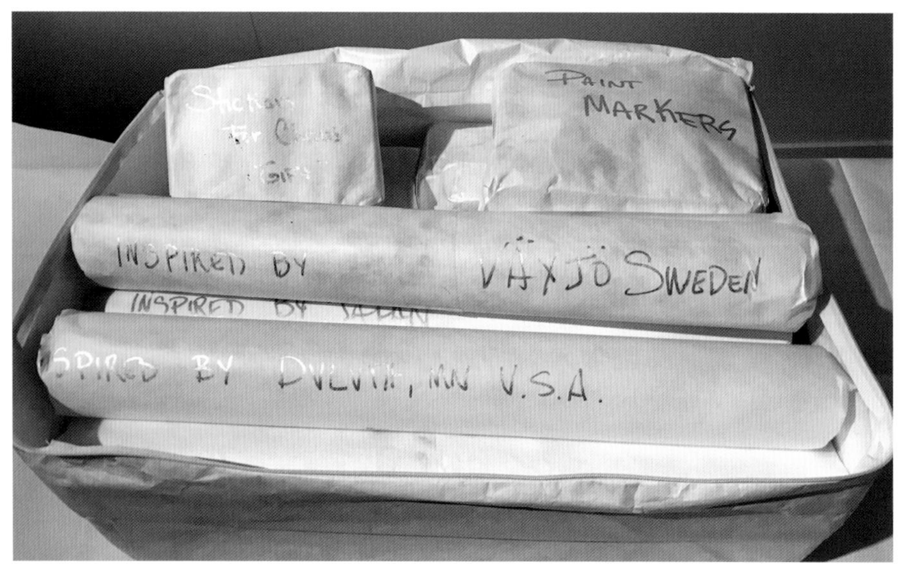

Top (left): Växjö Konsthall view from outside

Top (right): Amazing volunteers from Linnaeus University

Middle (left): Jennifer Phelps master roller in Labovitz studio preparing for Växjö exhibition

Middle (right): Anders Frazén, Skype interview, 2015

Bottom: Suitcase ready to travel containing white Tyvek® bag and entire exhibition for Växjö weighing under 45 pounds

Field Notes: Växjö, Sweden

March 4 – April 2, 2017 at Växjö Konsthall

Context

Two years after the Skype interviews between citizens of Växjö and myself, the exhibit at Växjö Konsthall became the third stop of the *122 Conversations* tour. More than 1,900 people came to the gallery during the exhibition. We had 20 school groups and held a family day with more than 300 people. I received this note from Filippa de Vos, Director of the Växjö Konsthall. *"Every time we use the gallery space for both reflections and physical activity I realize how knowledge is connected with body and mind. Also,* 122 Conversations *opened up for, if not global understandings, a common language through Anne's painted conversations and the additive work the audience made through the journey of the whole exhibition. It's great to see how an exhibition really grows over time by adding educational questions and methods to it."* For me Växjö was a deep and profound experience.

Process/Observations

Connecting with others to explore the ideals of humanity, and to practice the radical and political act of caring, are themes intentionally embodied in the work of the exhibition. The scrolls tell a story of connection — of conversations that reflect how similar we are while also celebrating our differences in thought, culture, and lived experience.

All touring venues enthusiastically embraced public engagement and offered educational opportunities. In turn, engagement and pedagogy became a central part of the project across all sites. In many places, and especially in Sweden, the participatory small works — some 500+ in all — were created by audience participants in response to both my artwork and the central tenets in the show. The exhibitions at each site were evolving, as was I. Traveling to Sweden seemed to accelerate the development of art education and workshops for the project. I arrived in Sweden in a cast due to a broken leg and spent long hours teaching daily ... but I didn't notice. I was inspired by so many people.

Reflections/Insight

In Sweden, I enhanced my existing pedagogy, developing it into a curriculum specific for *122 Conversations*. Here, I collaborated with UMD Art Education Professor Alison Aune, PhD to offer workshops to participants in Sweden and later in Duluth, using art to discuss human connection and cross-cultural dialogue. The aim of my pedagogy was to focus on seeing one another, as well as understanding the similarities and differences between us in relation to identity, geography, community, and culture through art. In Sweden, we worked alongside other art educators, with students, the public, and new immigrant groups, including refugees who had been in the country for only five days. *122 Conversations* literally opened up the gallery for a new audience. Many teachers in Växjö with whom we shared the pedagogy now use it in their classrooms. I'm thrilled that the ethos of the exhibition lives on and continues to be impactful through educators making it their own. I was fortunate enough to be asked to join Alison in March of 2017 to present on *122 Conversations* at the National Art Educators Association (NAEA) annual conference in Seattle. I will also be presenting to Art Educators of Minnesota (AEM) conference in November, 2018. I'm excited to share my experiences and pedagogy with educators.

A number of Duluth Sister Cities delegates traveled to the Sweden exhibition. They included Terese Tomanek, John Schmidt, Patti McGuire, Chelly Townsend, Gary Anderson, Gary Boelhower and Alison Aune. Student Parker Hinnenkamp brought the suitcase home to the U.S.A after the exhibition closed.

Participants

Anders Frazén, Annika Beckström, Ingemar Swalander and Berith Swalander, Matilda Bergstrand, Lena Wibroe, Gull-Britt Persson, Catherine Bringselius Nilsson, Fanny Geismar, and Åke Eriksson.

Gratitude Certificate of Participation, Petrozavodsk, 2015
Acrylic on Rives BFK paper
30" x 44"
Anne Labovitz

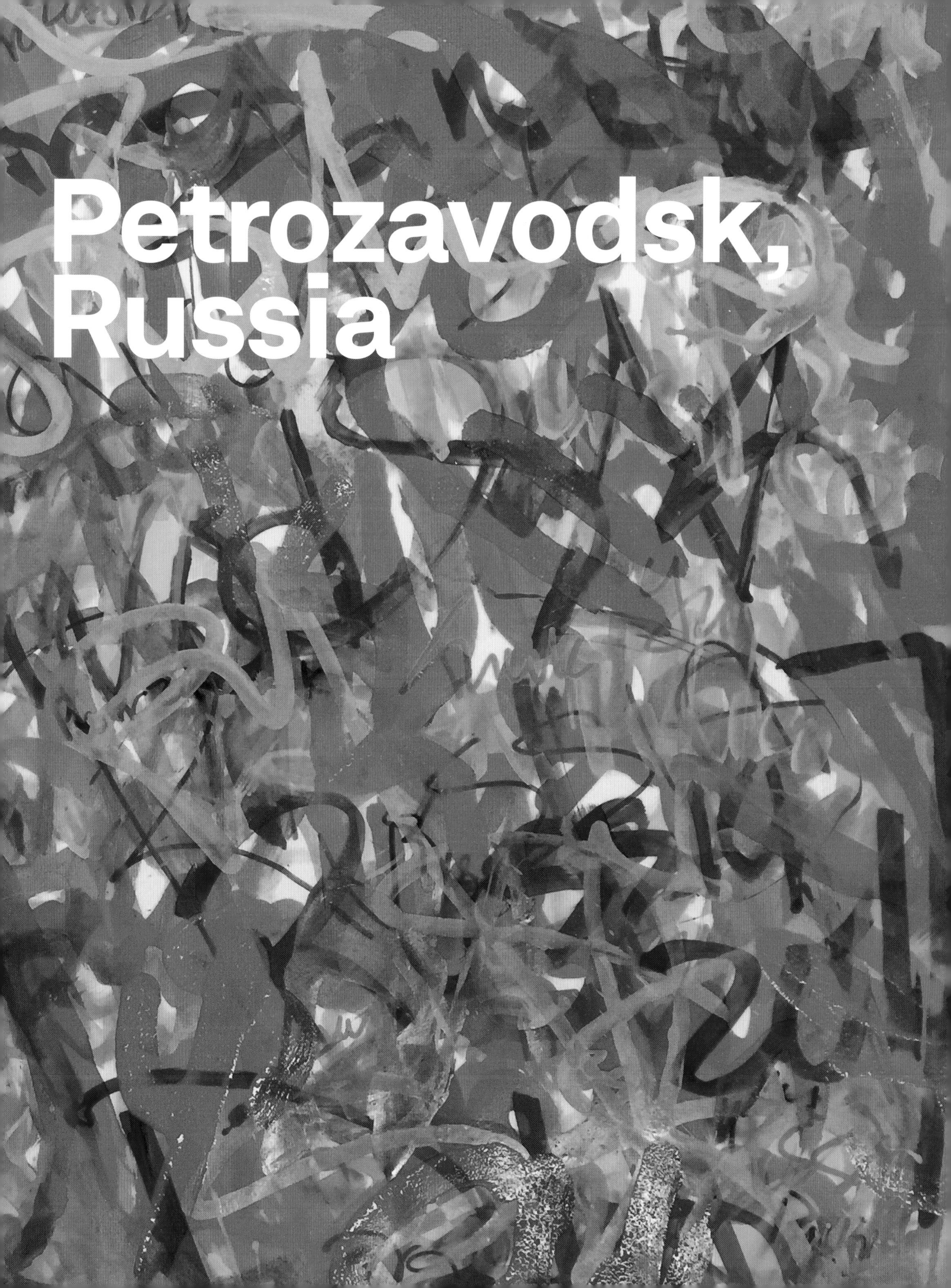

Petrozavodsk, Russia

Inspired by Thunder Bay for Russia, 2017
Acrylic on Tyvek®
Diptych 231.5" by 30" (left), 303.25" by 30" (right)
Anne Labovitz

Inspired by Växjö for Russia, 2017
Acrylic on Tyvek®
Diptych 321" by 30" (left), 301.5" by 30" (right)
Anne Labovitz

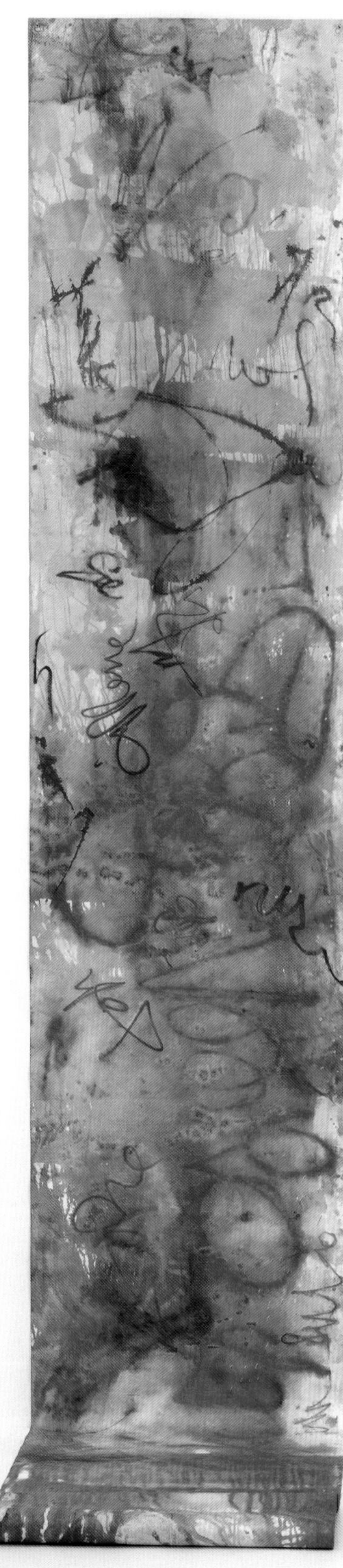

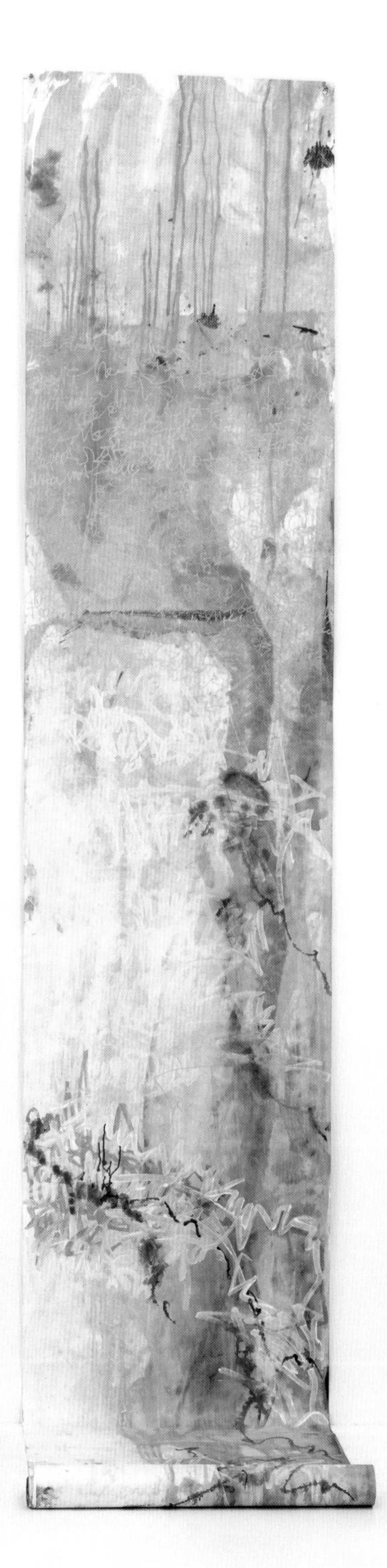

Inspired by Rania for Russia, 2017
Acrylic on Tyvek®
Diptych 324.5" by 30" (left), 328.5" by 30" (right)
Anne Labovitz

Inspired by Petrozavodsk for Russia, 2017
Acrylic on Tyvek®
Diptych 327.5" by 30" (left), 391.5" by 30" (right)
Anne Labovitz

Inspired by Petrozavodsk for Russia (detail), 2017
Acrylic on Tyvek®
327.5" by 30"
Anne Labovitz

Inspired by Ohara Isumi-City for Russia, 2017
Acrylic on Tyvek®
Diptych 327" by 30" (left), 309" by 30" (right)
Anne Labovitz

Inspired by Duluth for Russia, 2017
Acrylic on Tyvek®
Diptych 354" by 30" (left), 346.75" by 30" (right)
Anne Labovitz

Petrozavodsk City Exhibition Hall, installation, 2017

United Under the Night Sky, Petrozavodsk, 2017
Acrylic on Tyvek®
Diptych 396.5" by 30" (left), 401.75" by 30" (right)
Anne Labovitz
(permanent collection City of Petrozavodsk)

Large Choices Apron, Petrozavodsk (2), 2017
Stickers on Tyvek® with thread
50.5" by 45.75"
Anne Labovitz with Suy Path

Page 94/95:
Choices Tiles, Petrozavodsk, 2017
Acrylic on Tyvek®
8" by 5" each
Anne Labovitz with Citizens of Petrozavodsk

Art instructor with apron and student, Petrozavodsk, 2017

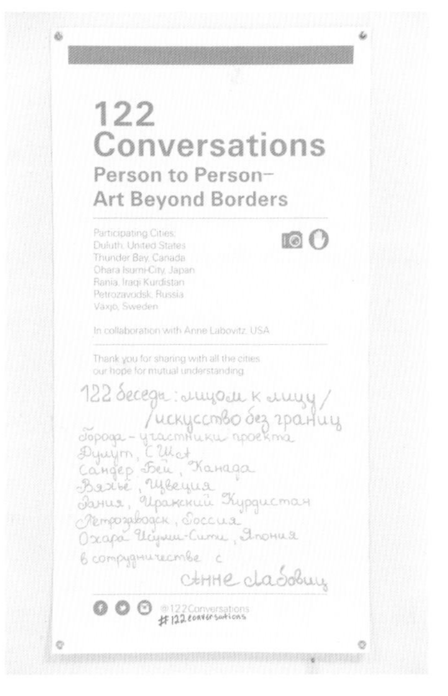

Top (left and right): Participants in Petrozavodsk

Middle (left): Margarita Bekirova in front of Petrozavodsk City Exhibition Hall

Middle (middle): Student with *Choices* tile

Middle (right): Translated banner in Petrozavodsk

Bottom: Duluth photographs by Jennifer Labovitz installed in Petrozavodsk

Top (left): Photographer Boris Konanov Skype interview, 2015

Top (right): Interviewees Natalya Lavrushina, Igor Krasnov, and Vadim Pavlov holding *Gratitude Certificates of Participation* at the opening, 2017

Middle (left): Denis Kozlov, Elena Magnitskaya, Skype interview 2015

Middle (right): Vera Meshko interpreter and interviewee via skype 2015

Bottom: Dan Noland and Devan Burnett

Field Notes: Petrozavodsk, Russia

May 25 – June 17, 2017 at Petrozavodsk City Exhibition Hall

Context

For two months in 2015, I conducted Skype interviews with the citizens of Petrozavodsk, Russia assisted by Vera Meshko. Similar to Rania and Växjö, these interviews were conducted to accommodate local time, often in the middle of the night! The city hosted the fourth venue on the *122 Conversations* exhibition tour. I received this note from Maria Yufa, director of the City Exhibition Hall about the show: *"Warm greetings to you from Petrozavodsk. The exhibition is successfully over. During the 19 days of its work it has been visited by 501 people, including: 108 children, 150 students, and 243 grown-ups. Several events were held by us, including: 1 opening ceremony, 8 concerts, 2 master-classes for children, 1 excursion."*

Process/Observations

In response to the high ceilings of the exhibition site at Petrozavodsk, I enlarged the scrolls to 30" wide by 25' long. This allowed for the intentional spooling of the scrolls on the floor. Metaphorically, we might think that the art, and the dialogue between myself and Russian citizens, could go on, and on, and on — held safe in the abstract colors of the artwork.

In addition, the Russian Sister City organizers requested 50 photographs for display. I selected 28 photos by Minnesota photographer Jennifer Will Labovitz of Duluth and 27 images from previous *122 Conversations* traveling activities. These photographs helped to further humanize the environment of display. *Note: I used an encompassing 22 foot long assemblage of such photographs in the Duluth venue.* The photographs prepared for the Petrozavodsk venue have since been scheduled to travel in Russia to Derzhavisky Lyceum (which has programs in cooperation with the Duluth's Marshall school).

Petrozavodsk is in northwest Russia, north of both St Petersburg and Moscow. Like Duluth, Petrozavodsk is a city on a great body of water — Lake Onega — which is the second-largest lake in Europe. I was unable to go to Russia, so a courier was needed. The rolling black suitcase once again came in handy. Thankfully, it was hand-delivered by Devan Burnett and facilitated by UMD Assistant Professor Dan Nolan. A thank you also goes to Neil Glazman, current Duluth Sister City Board Chair, who carried the suitcase exhibition back to Duluth.

Reflections/Insight

I was thinking about the nature of language and history as silent factors of influence in the course of developing my ideas about cross-cultural social engagement. Poet and feminist Adrienne Rich wrote that "a place on the map is also a place in history." I deeply wanted to address this truth and considered that language in and of itself is a vehicle. Not that language needs to be translated, but how language is learned, not taught. If we think of words and conversation in this way, we can begin to understand another person's use of language is as much a form of their sense of expression as it is a transmitter of specificity. I wondered about learning and understanding as a form of absorption outside of the words themselves. I felt something during the many Skype interviews that seemed to impart meaning in spite of the apparent awkwardness of waiting for translators' efforts to clarify the answers to questions. There was another aspect of sharing and understanding; the hearing and learning of each other. Seen first as a challenge for communication in the earlier venues of Rania, Iraqi Kurdistan; Växjö, Sweden; and again later in Ohara Isumi-City, Japan, the nature of language became a perceptual connector in Russia as well as a poignant signpost of stages of a relationship. I wondered: How can we understand each other better? *122 Conversations* poses some answers through dialogue, through creativity, and through color.

Recognizing the logistical challenges of language I am deeply grateful to each site's Sister City organization that managed translations of all textual material including labels, project descriptions, publicity, and signage. This service greatly enriched the program's ability to describe, engage, and encourage audience participation.

Participants

Yulia Parusova, Galina Shirshina, Vadim Pavlov, Boris Konanov, Vera Meshko, Elena Malysheva, Denis Kozlov, Elena Magnitskaya, Olga Klevina, Vladimir Lobanov, and Igor Krasnov.

Gratitude Certificate of Participation, Ohara Isumi-City, 2015
Acrylic on Rives BFK
30" by 44"
Anne Labovitz

Ohara
Isumi–City,
Japan

Inspired by Duluth for Japan, 2017
Acrylic on Tyvek®
Diptych 439.5" by 30" (left), 422" by 30" (right)
Anne Labovitz
(Right scroll private collection in Japan)

Inspired by Ohara Isumi-City for Japan, 2017
Acrylic on Tyvek®
Diptych 385" by 30" (left), 368" by 30" (right)
Anne Labovitz
(Right scroll private collection in Japan)

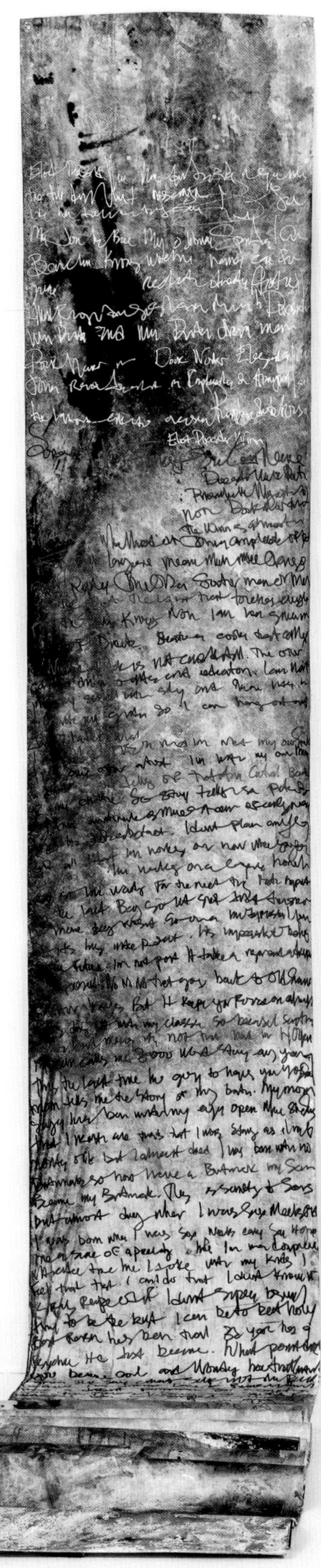

Inspired by Petrozavodsk for Japan, 201
Acrylic on Tyvek®
Diptych 415.5" by 30" (left), 389.25" by 30" (right)
Anne Labovitz

Inspired by Rania for Japan, 2017
Acrylic on Tyvek®
Diptych 415.5" by 30" (left), 410" by 30" (right)
Anne Labovitz

Tyvek® *Bag*, 2017
Tyvek® with thread and zipper
31" by 18" by 11"
Anne Labovitz with Suy Path

Inspired by Thunder Bay for Japan, 2017
Acrylic on Tyvek®
Diptych 442.5" by 30" (left), 400" by 30" (right)
Anne Labovitz

Inspired by Växjö for Japan, 2017
Acrylic on Tyvek®
Diptych 396.5" by 30" (left), 347.5" by 30" (right)
Anne Labovitz

Isumi-City Hall, installation, 2017

United Under the Night Sky, Ohara Isumi-City, 2017
Acrylic on Tyvek®
Diptych 452" by 30" (left), 445" by 30" (right)
Anne Labovitz

Large Choices Apron, Ohara Isumi-City (1), 2017
Acrylic on Tyvek® with thread
49.5" by 45"
Anne Labovitz with Suy Path

Page 114/115
Choices Tiles, Ohara Isumi-City, 2017
Acrylic on Tyvek®
7" by 4" each
Anne Labovitz with Citizens of Ohara Isumi-City

LOVE
and
Happy
Jill Lakhan
72
English
I have 3 children
+ 3 grandchildren
I live on a hill
by a big lake
ありがとう
Happy
Happy
Happy
Anne-San,
Thanks for
brightening
up our city!
These works
remind me of
koinobori, carp
streamers.
Thank you.
Rob Patt
LOVE & Smile
愛夢人好
侍富土山米
平和
繁栄
友情
Koji
毎日を感謝
幸福の
Happy!
Peace!
外国に行ってみたい
Teresa
Chaplain
Come back to
Ohara City!
手が描けるよう
外国行ってみたーい！

Eiko Ishii
I Love you!
なほ
You brought
such big artworks
of Love.
Aiko
LOVE
Thank you
Love & Peace
Love & Peace
naomi
Love you
all!
Naomi
楽しみにしています
がんばれ!!
いすみ市
I HOPE TO SEE YOU AGAIN. Isumi City You Have Been So Kind!
Wonderful drawings
Thank you very very
much Anne
Alice
感謝
Thanks
Anne!!
HOPE
In peace!
Thank you
Merci
Takk
Danke
謝謝
Hello!
你好
山崎 Family
with Love
see you
next time
また会いましょう
Kayo
My name is
Gale Kerns,
& I live in
Duluth, MN,
Isumi City's
Sister City
THANK
YOU
Y. YAMA
Yamazaki
Rie
wellcome
to isumi
Leaving our
♡'s
in Isumi City
I want to speak English
very well
I want to go Duluth.
YUKO
A Relationship
is a Power for
Peace
&
Happy
EMMA
大切な人が
ずっとずっと
幸せであるように!!
森優子
my name
Mio
優里子

Participant with color tile she created, *Choices*, Ohara Isumi-City, 2017

Top (left): Formal celebration post exhibition in office of Mayor Hiroshi Ota

Top (right): Student of Pavel Ishii and Daiki Santou wrote a thank you note

Middle (left): My Japanese family: Nao Ishii, Eiko Ishii, Reo Ishii, Labovitz, Daiki Santou, and Pavel Ishii. Amazing team effort for my two weeks in Japan

Middle (right): Middle school students in the studio

Bottom (left): Daiki Santou, Labovitz, and Mayor Hiroshi Ota

Bottom (right): Middle school student in the studio

姉妹都市（ダルース市）交流
アン・ラボヴィッツアート展
平成二十九年十月三十日～十一月三十日
ANNE・
LABOVITZ

Top (left): Duluth delegation and their counterparts with city officials opening *122 Conversations* in Isumi City

Top (right): Pavel Ishii, preparing to hang the scrolls with the bamboo he cut from his yard to serve as the spools from the top

Middle (left): Artist book created by Japanese photographer Kazutomo Kobayashi in Isumi city

Middle (center): Exhibition banner

Middle (right): Daiki Santou, Anne Labovitz, and Pavel Ishii collaboration piece, public park, Isumi City

Bottom: Children painting on scroll at public festival, Ohara Isumi-City

Field Notes: Ohara Isumi-City, Japan

November 1 – 30, 2017 at Isumi City Hall

Context

Like participants in Thunder Bay and Duluth, I interviewed the Japanese delegation of Sister City International in person in 2015. We met at the gorgeous and historically significant Glensheen Mansion in Duluth. These artworks travelled to Japan, as the fifth venue of the *122 Conversations* exhibition tour. There the exhibition was viewed by more than 500 people per day as they passed through their town's spacious civic building. Isumi City Hall turned out to be not only the most publicly available venue to date, but its high ceilings and vast atrium allowed for an exceptionally dramatic presentation of the scrolls, including their unfurling as part of the opening ceremony. Reporting onsite was Koresh Lakhan, *"In Isumi City folks looked up to the balcony in awe as the banners from the five Sister Cities were unfurled one at a time. Some described them as 'waterfall rainbows' and wished they would be there permanently."*

Process/Observations

A note from Eddie Crawford, Duluth Sister Cities delegate, expressed both his feelings about the project as well as his observations during the reveal of the show:

"122 Conversations *symbolizes the importance of our common understanding and appreciation of the world through art. It is a universal language that transmits into ONE common interest. One language that speaks volumes through our own intrapersonal and interpersonal understanding of the world... as well as through our life's experiences. The one by one unveiling of each painting was breathtaking. The 'tapestry' of people who were standing in the couloir of city hall in Ohara Isumi-City, [there] to observe and experience the unveiling of these beautiful and colorful paintings, appeared to revel in this delightful and magical revelation. Art inspires us all to focus on our common good and interest; mindful of who we are as a people and less apprehensive about the culture or the part of the world we live in."*

Reflections/Insight

Japan changed my practice. My work became an interweaving of artwork and public spaces. It was the first time I had worked at this scale in a public realm. *122 Conversations* escaped the confines of a formal gallery space to directly connect with citizens of Ohara Isumi-City. It was exhilarating — an immediate connection with the public; a type of socially engaged practice that I had been exploring. With the enormous amount of available space — three floors' high — the scrolls were made even longer than before — 30 inches wide by 35 feet long. In retrospect, the Japan scrolls represent not only the evolution of my art practice over the period of the six years, but also a drastically different perspective regarding how my artwork can occupy and engage with space as compared to the four-square paintings of Thunder Bay.

I visited Japan as an artist-in-residence, connecting and creating with a vast network of artists and educators. I collaborated with Pavel Ishii and Daiki Santou to create a black and white scroll, which was created at public interventions during several festivals. I directly connected to many Japanese communities and lived with a local artist's Japanese family. They accompanied me everywhere; I felt so special. It was such an intimate, personal, and creative experience; space was created for me to form a pathway for intimacy despite the language barrier. Oh, and those Japanese paints and brushes... amazing.

Duluth Sister Cities delegates who traveled and participated in the exhibition were Koresh and Jill Lakhan, Mary Hoffman, Terese Tomanek and Steve Davis, Irina Haller, Eddie Crawford, Dan Rau and Jeri and Gale Kerns.

Participants

Wakako Shoji, Sachiko Endo, Setuko Ishikawa, Kayo Nagano, Hayato Shoji, Tsukasa Kuga, Tomomi Takiguchi, Yukihiro Deguchi, Hiromichi Asano, and Koichi Uezima.

Sekaido art supply, new materials!

Gratitude Certificate of Participation, Duluth, 2015
Acrylic on Rives BFK
30" by 44"
Anne Labovitz

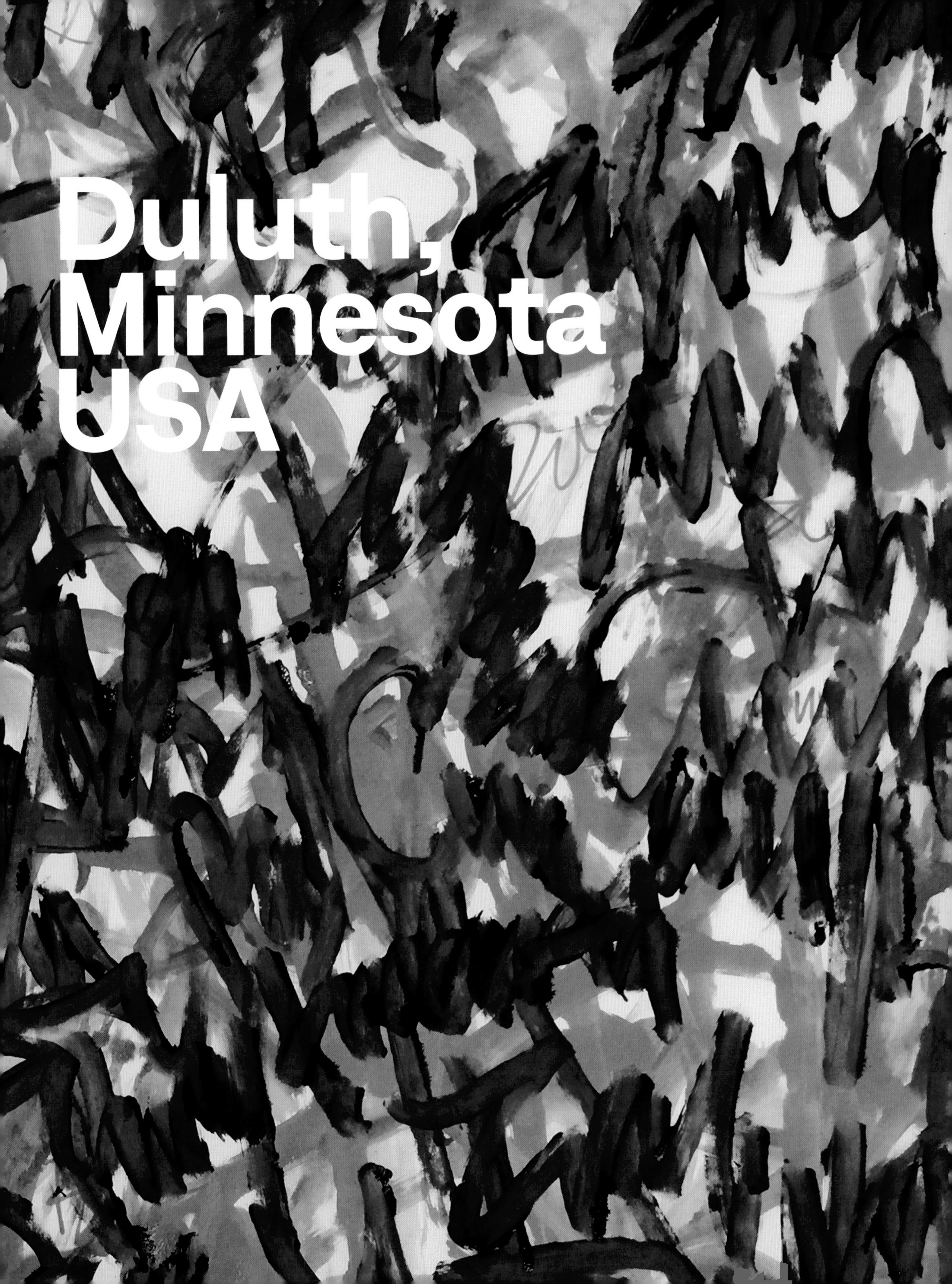
Duluth,
Minnesota
USA

Inspired by Ohara Isumi-City for Duluth, 2018
Acrylic on Tyvek®
Diptych 478.5" by 30" (left), 493" by 30" (right)
Anne Labovitz

Inspired by Petrozavodsk for Duluth, 2018
Acrylic on Tyvek®
Diptych 473.5" by 30" (left), 467" by 30" (right)
Anne Labovitz

Inspired by Rania for Duluth, 2018
Acrylic on Tyvek®
Diptych 473" by 30" (left), 505" by 30" (right)
Anne Labovitz

Inspired by Thunder Bay for Duluth, 2018
Acrylic on Tyvek®
Diptych 510" by 30" (left), 508.5" by 30" (right)
Anne Labovitz

Inspired by Thunder Bay for Duluth (detail), 2018
Acrylic on Tyvek®
508.5" by 30"
Anne Labovitz

... to ... up and ...

... fit at the ... I dont know ...

... to that was ... So back to the

equation, my Mom Sharon Ann Labowitz Provinske is the most generou

... This is a deep rooted value she embodies that

... part of my practice. She always shared ...

... the ... a gesture of kindness consideration and ...

Praxis. The relational exchange is very important

Cutting up paintings specifically created as gifts

... of a ... Crafts ... cards ... hand made

... collage; place into envelopes. The amount of time,

... thought about ... trying to understand it. I thrive

... studio on the shore of Lake Superior. And ...

Within me as an artist. I love to share

... any ... I love to ... to it

Person to Person ART BEYOND BORDERS was

40 inch paintings about ... created on ...

... one in the moment they were ...

... as a ... Thought ...

... there ... away to ... [illegible]

... is too complex art has too many ...

... the ... and ... But so ...

... the mission of ... [illegible]

Inspired by Växjö for Duluth, 2018
Acrylic on Tyvek®
Diptych 501.5" by 30" (left), 596.5" by 30" (right)
Anne Labovitz

Inspired by Duluth for Duluth, 2018
Acrylic on Tyvek®
Diptych 410.5" by 30" (left), 323" by 30" (right)
Anne Labovitz

Tweed Museum of Art, installation, 2018

United Under the Night Sky, Duluth, 2018
Acrylic on Tyvek®
Diptych 487.25" by 30" (left), 497" by 30" (right)
Anne Labovitz

Large Choices Apron, Duluth (2), 2018
Acrylic on Tyvek®
49" by 45"
Anne Labovitz with Suy Path

Page 134/135
Choices Tiles, Duluth, 2018
Acrylic on Tyvek®
6" by 6" each
Anne Labovitz with Citizens of Duluth

All the Beauty in this Whole Life
Peace for all
Duluth - like coming home
To the guy who smiled at me and my mom today. Thank you we had cried all morning
Champagne is Art
MATTER
Think Positive
Be Happy
Peace Frihet
YO ADRIAN I DID IT
Love the world and all its inhabitants
YOU ARE BRAVER Than YOU Think
Det Som fattas är hurdan man är - inte vem man är!
Good luck Brother Scott Oct 9th 2018 We Love you
Tack för all kärlek
Beethoven painted love through music - these paintings show a symphony in color that translates into Love and kindness
Allan
YOUR HEART SHINES BRIGHTER THAN THE DIAMONDS YOU'LL GET COMPARED TO YOUR MIND HOLDS MORE POWER THAN ANY HAND YOU'LL EVER HOLD AND YOUR VOICE SHAKES AND BREAKS THE WALLS BUILT AROUND YOU.
Natten är dagens mor. Kaos är granne med Gud!
Save the Boundary Waters
I can't explain what I mean. And even if I could, I'm not sure I'd feel like it...
one tiny blue marble
HOME
May you LIVE in your LIGHT thoughts and LEARN from your DARK

only one
the way
you do.
BREATHE
the things we LOVE TELL US what we are
St. Thomas Aquinas
Miigwetch
Mino-Bimaadiziwin
Take care of your heart!
Be Kind
It matters
We're ALL Connected!
LANGUAGE OF
NOTHING LEFT TO DO BUT SMILE, SMILE, SMILE
my friends get me excited! fired up! I ♡ you girls thanks for always having my back
Being Different is Beautiful
amour
ensemble
relation amicale
Breath
Stance
JOY
Love your Neighbor
Let there Be Peace
You are more than good Enough
I came From the Cities Hopefully I can Make this my Home
和
МИР
Peace
Miigwetch
You Have My Whole ♡...
The silence after the rain... how quickly the SKY pulls itself together.
Water is Life
Every event will have meaning Focus on the POSITIVE!

Interviewee Sarah Curtis creating at Tweed

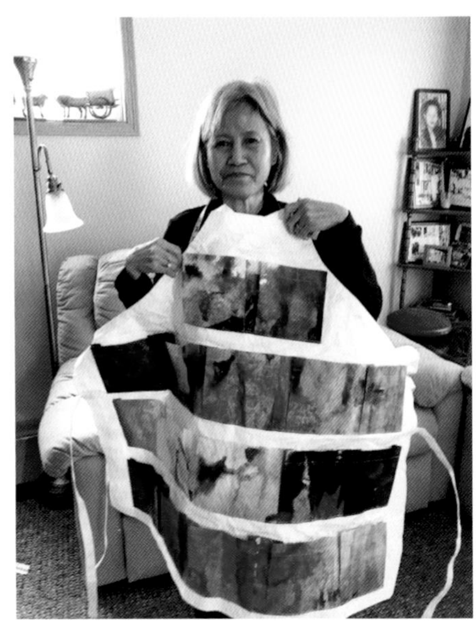

Top (left): *Choices* wall at Tweed Museum of Art with student

Top (right): Suy Path, master seamstress with one of the many aprons she sewed

Middle (left): Terese Tomanek and Steve Davis finding their photos on the photo wall, Tweed Museum of Art

Middle (right): Monica Sandberg amazing coordinator of Swedish delegation, Tweed Museum of Art

Bottom (left): Duluth Sister Cities Board meeting via Skype 2015

Bottom (right): UMD student group from Public health

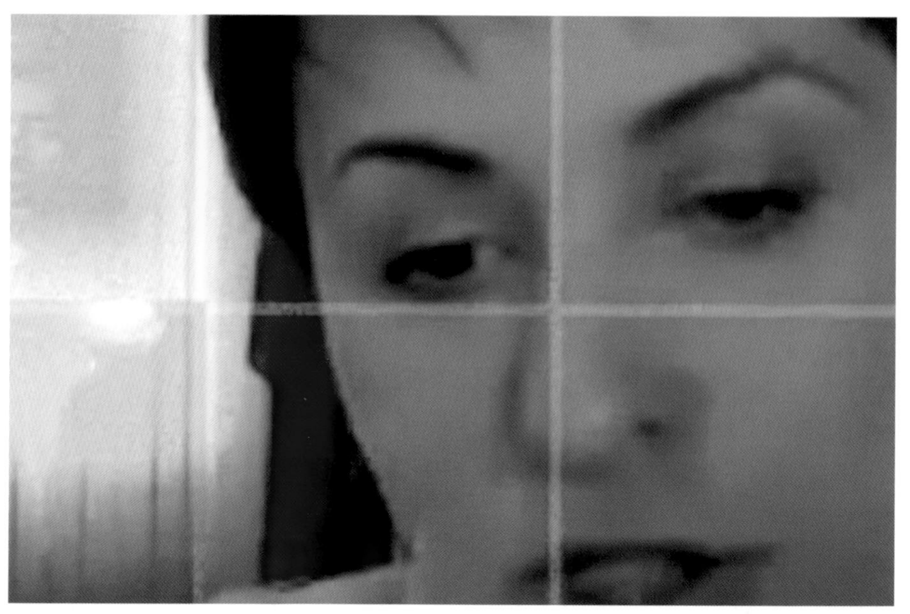

Top (left): Crystal Lohman, DSCI, 2015

Top (right): Still from *Mayors' Video*, 56 minutes, Anne Labovitz, 2017. Interview with previous mayor of Petrozavodsk, Galina Shirshina.

Middle (left): Mayor Larson a great supporter of *122 Conversations*, Tweed Museum of Art, 2018

Middle (center): Prototype *Peace* necklace created by Labovitz in collaboration with Security Jewelers

Middle (right): Note from young person at Fourth Fest Duluth, 2015

Bottom: Swedish delegation and Sister Cities representatives at Tweed Museum of Art, 2018

Field Notes: Duluth, Minnesota, USA

September 25, 2018 – January 6, 2019 at the Tweed Museum of Art, University of Minnesota – Duluth

Context

The sixth and final venue of the *122 Conversations* tour is at the University of Minnesota Duluth Tweed Museum of Art. Duluth is my hometown and where this entire crazy, imaginative, and complex project was envisioned. Over the past six years audience participants have painted, drawn, and marked in some imaginative way more than 2,500 small works (tiles) called *Choices*. In partnership with my paintings, *Choices* toured six countries. Mind blowingly, more than 3,000 people volunteered for this project (more to come in Duluth).

In 2015, I interviewed representatives of the Duluth Sister City organization for this project. But that was not the beginning. Since 2012, I have been encouraging, supporting, and gathering energy and people for support.

Process/Observations

An important part of the project was the development of the work physically and conceptually. How does an artist capture the multitude of identities, cultures, thoughts, hopes, and dreams of many people into one painting? Over the course of 2014-15, I developed the work through experimenting with projects devised for various public engagements. These prototype projects included an all-night interactive painting performance at the Weisman Art Museum of the University of Minnesota Twin Cities during the Northern Spark Art Festival, and the Rain Taxi Book Festival at the State Fairgrounds where I created a bookmark exchange project.

Reflections/Insight

Now 2,000+ artworks comprise the work of people from six countries. By the end of the Tweed Museum show more than 2,500 will have been made! Reflecting on the whole project and considering the work in its entirety, I feel the scrolls embody the *122 Conversations* ideas as a compilation of the discussions via Skype; the pocketed aprons worn by volunteers offering tiles for participants to make *Choices* represent a visual gesture that reflects the encounter and excitement of so many people; and the grids reflect the intense and emotional interaction with audiences in each of the Sister Cities. All of this amounts to a radical act of caring shared by thousands.

As with every other exhibition in *122 Conversations*, the Duluth-based program will evolve over time. At Tweed, an activity room/project space has been appointed with plenty of artmaking materials. I hope hundreds of people will contribute as others have by creating their own color tile to express their take on the show's themes.

The mayor of Duluth, Emily Larson, attended the opening along with Swedish delegates from Växjö: Marie-Louise Gustavsson, Lena Wibroe, Monica Sandberg, Lennart Johansson, Gunnel Holmér and RosMarie Jönsson Neckö.

Participants

Don Ness, Cheng Khee Chee, Renee Passal, Sarah Curtiss, Traci Marciniak, Anne Tanski, Rob Link, Dan Hartman, Gordon Ramsay, and Jireh Mababamba

Labovitz received the key to all 5 sister cities in recognition for her work with *122 Conversations*, Duluth 2015

Anne Labovitz studio

Anne Labovitz

In 2012, I was inspired by the Sister City International mission: "To promote peace through mutual respect, understanding, and cooperation — one individual at a time." These ideas resonated with me, as my practice for the past 30 years has been about the human spirit, its emotional resonance, and the way it manifests in relationships. The following six years I developed and executed a project with collaborators embodying these principles. These years have been ones of transformation, generosity, friendship, and intense research into engaging in radical acts of caring. *122 Conversations: Person to Person, Art Beyond Borders* is a creative series that encompassed an artist-led research project, a six-venue exhibition tour, more than a dozen social practice interventions, 20+ workshops, and numerous lectures convened over six years, four continents, and six countries.

I create portraiture in the broadest sense. My work has often captured a human element — a figure, a mark, a word — as well as representing a portrait of place. Regularly, I employ painting, drawing, printmaking, experimental film, and performative participatory art. Recently, I have incorporated text, audience engagement, alternative materials, and public interventions as vital elements of my praxis, elements all included in *122 Conversations*.

Working with Sister City friends has bolstered my optimism and strengthened my beliefs in our shared humanity. The importance of inclusion and honoring differences are values I embrace. I strive to utilize language, dialogue, and art as vehicles to portray these values. These have directed, shaped, and guided the project.

The 60 interviews conducted and recorded are the core of this project and formed the source material. If unable to have dialogue in person, the interactions were via Skype. This reflects the use of the information age to create meaningful human connection in combination with the handwritten mark to shorten distances both literally and figuratively. I documented conversations of human connection, aiming to archive experiences and visually chronicle them through art as a universal language. I have learned, heard, and experienced astounding beauty and resilience within the arch of 60 interviews. Without exception, I fell in love....

Empathy and dialogue as process is embodied in *122 Conversations*. Together, we united our unique perspectives and visual languages to build contextual communities and acknowledge our shared humanity as citizens on the same planet. This project centers around connection and seeing each other, and as part of that I created *United Under the Night Sky*, seeking a common ground to unite us.

Utilizing imagery consisting of color, the written word, and at times the human form, I hope the pieces draw the viewer inward to experience an encounter with the subject and the collective consciousness. We have different religions, languages, geography, values, yet humanity binds us. Throughout the 60 interviews, people across six countries hoped for a better world for their children; they hoped their children finished their studies; and there was a unifying hope for peace. We are all vulnerable. We all have compassion. People want their stories to be shared and understood.

I approached the creation of the paintings with the same rigor, intent, focus, and mindfulness that I employed while conducting the interviews themselves. I felt a sense of obligation, as well as creative intentionality. As I revisited my experiences with each participant, I focused on embedding the painting with the essence of the subject's beauty, resilience, and spirit as well as their connection to the other interviewees through overlapping layers.

Color can be an emotive connector. My use of it is driven both by process and intuition. Some colors are chosen as a result of my response to the re-listening of the interview, others are chosen with consideration of more formal elements of composition and contrasting tone. In this way, each piece acquires its uniqueness reflecting the essence of the conversations.

My grandmother, Ella Labovitz, often talked about Martin Buber's "I Thou" philosophy, describing it as a pause between humans where we see each other and all else fades away. Extrapolating from this, the artwork and, in particular, the tiles offer a neutral place for the exchange of stories, ideas, and drawings submitted by participants at each venue.

I hope people who read this catalog will feel the presence of the more than 3,000 humans who volunteered their time and shared their stories to come together in the spirit of community.

122 Conversations is an artist-led project based on the art of engagement and derived from interconnection and cross-cultural dialogue. This project celebrates humanity, human connection, and the radical and political act of caring. The project is metaphorically a global, visual chorus celebrating our differences and a place for people to participate, joining the chorus.

Anne Labovitz / CV

Anne Labovitz is an American artist based in St. Paul, Minnesota, whose practice includes painting, drawing, and printmaking as well as experimental film and performative participatory works. Her work considers many themes often returning to the central notion of an enduring interest in people. Working within the portraiture tradition, she employs a process of layering — from multiple images and text to conceptual connections and multiple elements of physicality found in mark-making and materiality. She exhibits nationally and internationally.

Education
2017: MFA Plymouth University, UK/ Transart Institute, Berlin, Germany/ New York City, USA | **1989**: BA Art and Psychology, Minor Art Education & Art History, Hamline University, St. Paul, MN

Select Solo Exhibitions
2018: *122 Conversations,* Tweed Museum of Art, Duluth, MN | **2017**: *122 Conversations,* Ohara Isumi-City, Japan | *122 Conversations*, Rania, Iraqi Kurdistan, University of Raparin | *122 Conversations,* Växjo, Sweden, Konsthall | *122 Conversations,* Petrozavodsk, Russia | **2015**: *122 Conversations,* Thunder Bay Art Gallery, Thunder Bay, Canada | *Earth & Water,* Crary Art Gallery, Warren, PA, January 2015 | **2014**: *Layers,* Burnet Gallery, Le Méridien Chambers, Minneapolis, MN | **2013**: *Composite Portraits,* Tweed Museum of Art, Duluth, MN | **2010**: *Passions,* Athenaeum Music & Arts Library, La Jolla, CA | **2002–06**: *Anne Labovitz,* El Refor, Bilbao, Spain | **2002**: *Anne Labovitz,* Fine Arts Gallery, Arkansas State University, St. University, AK | *Anne Labovitz,* Chapman Art Center Gallery, Cazenovia College, Cazenovia, NY | *New Work by Anne Labovitz,* Talgut die Schönen, Künste, Germany | **1998**: *Hot off the Press,* Steve Powell Gallery, Taos, NM

Select Group Exhibitions
2018: *Let's Go Refreshed,* Burnet Fine Art & Advisory, Wayzata, MN | **2015**: *Someone Else's Story,* Burnet Gallery, Minneapolis, MN | **2013–14**: *Blood Memoirs,* Tweed Museum of Art, Duluth, MN. Curated by Amber-Dawn Bear Robe | Art Fair, Select Fair NYC, Frieze Week NYC, with Burnet Gallery, Minneapolis, MN | *Selections from the Permanent Collection,* Athenaeum Music & Arts Library, La Jolla, CA. Curated by Erica Torri | **2012**: *Anima,* Fibre Arts Design, Palo Alto, CA | **2011**: *INTERBIFEB XIV,* Gallerija Portreta, Tuzla, Bosnia-Herzegovinia | **2010**: *Pipe 10,* Penang State Art Gallery, Penang, Malaysia | National Association of Women Artists, NY, NY | **2006**: Kunstverein Neustadt e.v., Neustadt, Germany | **2002**: T.W. Wood Gallery & Art Center, Vermont College, Montpellier, VT | **1998**: Sanata Reporta, Florence, Italy | **1997**: Mostra, Commune Centrale, Barga, Italy | Taos Art Association, Taos, NM | **1995**: *Selected Group,* Finley Gallery, Birmingham, AL | *A Different Language,* New Masters Fine Arts, Taos, NM | **1994**: *Ella and Anne Labovitz,* Duluth Art Institute, Duluth, MN | Gallery 416, Minneapolis, MN

Publications
2013: *Anne Labovitz: Composite Portraits,* catalog, Tweed Museum of Art, June 2013 | Exhibition Catalog, Penang State Art Gallery, Penang, Malaysia | Studio Visit, Volume 19, curated by Jonathan Greene | *Selections from the Permanent Collection, 1990-2010,* Athenaeum Music & Arts Library, 2013 | **2011–12**: *International Contemporary Artists,* Vol. II and III | **2010**: *New American Paintings,* Midwest Region, No. 89, curated by Lisa Dorin | *Color Train,* artist book, collaboration with Bill Gamble | *Dungeon Depths: Two Artists Explore the Self-Portrait,* A. Labovitz and C. Best | **2009**: *A Dozen Days in the Dungeon,* A. Labovitz and C. Best | Honoral and Zarina, B. Gamble and A. Labovitz | **2007**: *Dwellings 2,* Labovitz and C. Best | **2004**: *Champagne Art Book,* A. Labovitz and C. Best

Collections
Work is held in numerous private and public collections. Public collections include: the Minnesota Historical Society, Minnesota Museum of American Art, St. Paul, MN, Frederick R Weisman Art Museum, Tweed Museum of Art, Univ. of MN, Duluth, MN, Athenaeum, La Jolla Ca, Duluth Women's Building, Duluth, MN, Studio Camnitzer, Lucca, Italy, City of Växjö, Sweden, and the University of Raparin, Rania, Iraqi Kurdistan. Corporate collections: Maurices, Duluth, MN, Baviera International, Stockholm, Sweden, Penang International Printmaking, Penang-Malaysia, Burr and Forman, Birmingham, AL, Piper Jaffray, Fargo, ND, Wells Fargo, Duluth, MN, Spezialarzt fur Innere Medizin FMH, Basil, Switzerland, and the Duluth Housing Authority, Duluth, MN. Private collections: Ralph and Peggy Burnet, Minneapolis, MN, Lyndel and Blaine King, Minneapolis, MN, and Dr. Hugo Steiner, Basel, Switzerland. Private collector in Japan.

A complete CV is available online at www.labovitz.com

Acknowledgements

First and foremost thank you to my entire family who guided me, supported me, and loved me through this odyssey and without whose fundamental help I would be adrift. Thank you for all your diligent committed hard work over the last six years: Katy Dieperink, Megan Arney Johnston, Jennifer Phelps, Joseph D.R. OLeary, Ken Bloom, and the Tweed Museum. To all the amazing committed volunteers of Duluth Sister Cities International past and present. Grateful to Darsie Alexander, Omayra Alvarado, and Jack Becker for their thoughtful consideration of my work and this project.

Thank you to Duluth Sister Cities International past and present board members, volunteers, and staff.

Venues

Thunder Bay Art Gallery, Thunder Bay, Ontario, Canada
Växjö Konsthall, Växjö, Sweden
Petrozavodsk Municipal Gallery, Petrozavodsk, Russia
University of Raparin, Rania, Iraqi Kurdistan
Isumi Civic Building, Ohara Isumi-City, Japan
Tweed Museum of Art, City of Duluth

Sponsors

City of Duluth
Duluth News Tribune
Holiday Inn Duluth
Hoops Brewery
Lyric Kitchen and Bar
Otis Magie
Security Jewelers
Visit Duluth

Organizations

DSCI (Duluth Sister Cities International)
Tweed Museum of Art
University of Minnesota, Duluth, School of Fine Arts
Sister City Organizations of: Växjö, Sweden; Thunder Bay, Canada; Rania, Iraqi Kurdistan; Petrozavodsk, Russia; Ohara Isumi-City, Japan
Rayal Center for Cultural Exchange
SCI (Sister City International)

Individuals

Dr. Harold Robinson Adams
Eleanor Albanese
Darsie Alexander
Khalil Ali Abdulla
Salah Ali Wais
Omayra Alvarado
Brooks Anderson
Gary Anderson
Peg Apka
Alison Aune
Kurdo Aziz Bagg
Sarah & Mick Bauer
Maya Li Bauer
Cecelia Bauer
Jack Becker
Annika Beckström
Pavel Bednar
Tammi Beier
Margarita Bekirova
Matilda Bergstrand
Lendley Black
Ken Bloom
Gary Boelhower
Catherine Bringselius Nilsson
Ola Brorson
Lisa Bravo
Devan Burnett
Elizabeth Buset
Christina Chang
Montgomery Chavez
Regina Christensen
Gary Cooper
Michael Cousino
Ed Crawford
Janice Crede
Eva Cronquist
Jill Custer
Josephine Dahlberg Jigander
Steve Davis
Filippa de Vos
Yukihiro Deguchi
Jean-Ulrick Désert
Katy Dieperink
Lauren Dieperink
Camille Doran
Michelle Dorosier
Damon Dowbak
Elliott Doxtater-Wynn
Robert Eady
Lauryn Eady
Meaghan Eley
Mark Emmel
Åke Eriksson
Denny Falk
Lisa Fitzpatrick
Dan Fitzpatrick
Angie Frank
Anders Franzén
Lillian Freemond
Bill Gamble
Henry, Isabella & Edward Gamble
Andrew Garrow
Fanny Geismar
Zoe Genova
Neil Glazman
Sharon Godwin
Andrew & Katarzyna Goode
Irina Haller
Niazy Hama Aziz
Ali Hammad Bagg
John Hannam
Jacqueline Hanson
Nicolas Hansson
Shigeru Harads
Dan Hartman
Rebwar Hazhar
Marv Heikkinen
Fletcher Hinds
Parker Hinnenkamp

Keith Hobbs
Mary Hoffman
Rob Hofmann
Beth Holst
Dave Hoops
Donna Howard
Will Hreb
Karissa Isaacs
Eiko Ishii
Reo & Nao Ishii
Megumi Itoh
Olga Ivanova
Salah Jamal Khurshid
Maija Jenson
Jennifer Johnson
Megan Arney Johnston
Arno Kahn
Robert Kase
Jeri & Gale Kerns
Kazutomo Kobayashi
Nyomie Korcheski
Judy Kresky
Lisa & Mike Kuberra
Nadia Kurd
Sharon & Joel Labovitz
Jennifer & Mark Labovitz
Ella & Maurice Labovitz
Katherine LaFleur
Koresh & Jill Lakhan
Rick Lang
Mayor Emily Larson
Natalya Lavrushina
Yukai Li
Rob Link
Mike Linn
Bronwyn Lipinski
Tom Livingston
Crystal Lohman
Eric Lorberer

Sharon Louden
Mihoko Lwata
Alistair Mackay
Bonnie Mackey
Faruq Mala Fatih
Laura McClean
Trista McGovern
Patti McGuire
Catherine Meier
Lori Melton
Vera Meshko
Patricia Miller
Shirwan Mirza
Nigar Mohammed Ali
Tom Morgan
Michelle Naar-Obed
Kayoko Nakajima
Roger Nash
Don Ness
David & Inga-Lill Newkumet
Dan Nolan
Danielle Norkunas
Ruth Novaczek
Trisha O'Keefe
Joseph D.R. OLeary
Carolyn Olson
Hiroshi Ota
Barb Palkki
Lars Palm
Jennifer Parker
Renee Passal
Suy Path
Bill Payne
Beth Peloff
Gull-Britt Persson
Glenn Peterson
Kathy Peterson
Jennifer Phelps
Gene Pittman

Alsace & Albert Provinske
Dan Rau
Linda Riddle
Wendy Ruhnke
Monica Sandberg
Kathy Sandstedt
Daiki Santou
Martin Schibli
John Schmidt
Jay Seiler
Layth Seyala
Suzanne Seyala
David Sherman
Wakako Shoji
Kirk Sklar
Erin Smith
Hannah Smith
Helen Smith Stone
Bart Snyder
Bill Sozanski
Jeff Stark
Tom Stark
Tom & Mimi Stender
Christine Strom
Ingemar & Berith Swalander
Tomo Takiguchi
Aki Tanizumi
Abi Tariq
Liz Taylor
Terese Tomanek
Laadona Torrnabene
Chelly Townsend
Emmy Vadnais
Christine Valento
Anneliese Verhoeven
Charlie Wagner
Elle-Andra Warner
Mulla Abdulla Wasman Adam
Jane Wattrus

Tim Wegren
Benny Weinbeck
Wendy Wennberg
Lena Wibroe
Lynne WIlliams
Gudrun Witrak
Vivian Wood-Alexander
Harmony Works
Wendy Wright
Ka Yang
Fumiyo Yonekawa
Masamichi Yoshino
Rubar Yousef
Maria Yufa
Tom Zelman
Khaled Qader
Golden Artist Colors support line

Thank you to everyone who helped make this project possible, alive, and breathing. If I have forgotten your name or did not get the opportunity to know your name, I am still grateful.